The Cost of You

The Cost of You

Financial Clarity in a World That Profits When You Are Confused

By Zack Fields

ISBN 979-8-9934119-4-1

First Edition

To my mom, thank you for years of support and for answering the random calls where I talked money, interrupting bridge and TV shows from 2,500 miles away.

Most people think they spend when they swipe.
But the spending starts before you even wake
up.

Introduction

I'm writing this on the edge of what feels like a recession—
not a crash, not a cliff, but something slower, more
corrosive. A downturn that echoes the grinding freeze after
Japan's asset bubble… or the quiet unraveling that followed the
Roaring Twenties. We're not watching things fall apart in
dramatic fashion—we're watching them wear down. Rent
inching up. Grocery trips doubling. Wages flatlining. It's death
by a thousand transactions.

Not the kind you choose—but the kind that choose you. Bills
that hit before you open your eyes. Fees you forgot. Charges
you didn't agree to. A system designed to make you spend
without noticing… and blame yourself when you do.

The headlines call it inflation or normalization. But the lived
reality? It's economic erosion. We're living through it.

And behind all of it sits policy—tariffs, trade shifts, and hidden
costs dressed up as patriotism. We keep getting told tariffs are
about strength or protecting American workers. Let's be real…
tariffs are just taxes on us, the consumers. Some of the biggest
we've seen in years. And they were voted in—picked with this
president—while Congress stood by and did nothing.

Economists love to measure motion—year over year, quarter
over quarter—as if that explains how people actually live. But
what if we measured distance instead of motion? Sixty years.
Three generations. The span between what our grandparents
could afford and what we can't. If economics tracked that
distance, we'd see how far we've drifted… and how broken the
story really is.

People love to quote Adam Smith's "invisible hand," as if
markets magically correct themselves. But Smith himself spent
more time writing about morality than markets. His first book—
The Theory of Moral Sentiments—wasn't about profit, but about
empathy and community. That part of his work is often ignored,

leaving behind a myth that self-interest alone would carry society forward.

Why This Book Matters Now

My goal with this book is simple: I want to give people a financial model that actually works. One they can use for the rest of their lives. Not just to save money—but to reclaim control. Especially now, in a time when the safety nets are thinning, credit card debt is at an all-time high, and the systems we were told to trust are leaving more and more people behind. Because let's be honest: most of those systems were never built with you in mind.
They were built to extract. To confuse.
The final twist? They make you feel like the struggle was your fault.

We've seen this movie before. Over a century ago, during America's first Gilded Age, wealth pooled at the top, politicians worked for tycoons, and workers had little power to fight back. What followed was decades of reform—trust-busting, labor laws, and taxes that rebuilt the middle class.

That era taught us that concentrated power doesn't correct itself —it only shifts when people demand it.

Today, we're living through a second Gilded Age. The wealth gap is wider than ever, corporate power is concentrated, and the average person is left navigating a rigged system designed to drain—not build—financial stability.

This book is here to challenge that. Because what we're really fighting isn't just income inequality or inflation—it's extraction. The slow, systematic siphoning of your time, your energy, and your money.

I say that as a millennial who's already seen the dot-com collapse, the Great Recession, and whatever this is shaping up to be. I've watched peers crushed by student loans. I've watched families lose homes. I've watched coworkers burn themselves out trying to "earn more" when the real secret was learning how to need less.

I've watched wealth concentrate in a way that no budget book dares to address—because calling it out would mean admitting that this isn't just about math. It's about power.

From Budgeting to Bigger Truths

Originally, this book was going to be about budgeting. The spreadsheet kind. I planned to teach you the same model that's helped me, a roommate, an ex, and more than a handful of friends avoid debt, build savings, and stop dreading the end of the month. It was going to focus on the micro-level tools of financial literacy—daily spend tracking, interest rate awareness, saving intentionally. The kind of practical stuff most people were never taught.

But somewhere along the way, I realized something bigger: this is what financial literacy should actually look like. Not just math and money—but power, awareness, systems, and behavior. Real-world, lived-in, non-boring financial literacy. The kind we all should've had from the start.

We'll still get to that. But as I wrote, it became obvious: budgeting is just one piece.

Because in this economy, you can do everything right and still fall short. You can work hard, avoid debt, live below your means—and still feel like you're treading water.

Why? Because the real cost isn't just in the lattes. It's in the loans. The housing. The decisions that last a decade. That's where people fall behind—and no spreadsheet is going to fix that by itself.

So this isn't just a budgeting book. It's a book about the bigger picture. About the system we live in… and how to survive inside it. Especially when that system rewards overspending, punishes caution, and convinces you it's all your fault when things go wrong.

The Cruel Setup

Let's be honest. The average American is expected to navigate life like they have a PhD in capitalism and a minor in socialism —while never actually being taught how either works.

We're supposed to optimize retirement plans, understand compound interest, negotiate salaries, avoid predatory loans, pick the right insurance, build credit, refinance debt, avoid bankruptcy… and still somehow feel guilty when we get it wrong.

It's a cruel setup. One designed to make failure feel personal— when most of the damage was engineered into the system from the start.

Meanwhile, while we're trying to Google our way to stability, institutions are cashing in. Confusion is profitable. Complexity is intentional. And shame? Shame is the engine. It keeps you quiet. It keeps you compliant. It keeps you from realizing that this isn't just your fault—it's your environment.

Financial mistakes aren't always about irresponsibility. Sometimes they're just about timing. Or desperation. Or trusting the wrong people. I've made mistakes. You will too. But this book is built to help you make fewer—and more importantly, to forgive yourself for the ones you've already made.
Because shame has never helped anyone climb out of debt. But clarity? Clarity can change your life.

The Bigger Picture

Just so we're clear from the jump—this book isn't just about your finances.

It's part of a broader vision. I believe that if we're ever going to build a more equitable country, we have to start with financial literacy. We have to take power back—one household at a time. This book is my blueprint, but it's also my launching pad. I want this message in schools. I want it in public service. I want it on stages, in workshops, in communities where economic pain has been normalized and passed down like furniture.

Because it's not just about budgeting—it's about dignity.

When people understand how their money moves, they start asking better questions. About housing. About healthcare. About taxes. About why billionaires pay less in percentage than their assistants. About why one medical bill can bankrupt a family, but corporate write-offs go untouched.

Those questions matter. Because the truth is, most of your financial struggle isn't about "bad choices." It's about living in a system that hides the real levers of power—and punishes you for not knowing they exist.

That's why I don't just see this as a fight for financial literacy—I see it as a fight against theft disguised as policy.
People say socialism is a redistribution of wealth. But for decades, we've lived through something far more dangerous: a quiet, relentless redistribution of theft—trillions flowing upward while we're told to budget harder.
This book is about reclaiming what was taken.

I'm not just writing this book to help you fix your money. I'm writing it because I believe that real change—the kind that rebalances power—starts with understanding how money works in your life and in your society.

The politicians won't save you. The Fed isn't coming down from the mountaintop to hand you a better APR. The era of free money is over unless we fall off an economic cliff. That's not cynicism. That's clarity. That's why building resilience, awareness, and financial flexibility matters more than ever before.

My Story

I got my MBA from UCLA Anderson. Before that, I studied marketing at Syracuse and played D1 lacrosse—mostly from the sidelines, but still. My career took me into corporate strategy, with a focus on housing, broadband, and competitive intelligence. I got paid to understand how people moved, disconnected services, and made financial decisions—especially at the end of the month.

That meant knowing when households were likely to cancel internet, when rent was going to be missed, and what signs predicted economic strain. It wasn't just numbers. It was empathy. Because I had been there too.

I started building my budget model back in 2011, born out of a mistake I made buying my first car.

It was a 2012 Volkswagen CC, released early in April 2011. By May, my first payment—just under $430—was due on the 20th. I paid it in full, and it cleared by the 22nd. But with rent and other bills coming due, I still had money left in my account. So, in my infinite wisdom, I thought: "Why not pay June early, while I have the money?"

What I didn't know was that Volkswagen's system wouldn't recognize the early payment as covering June. It processed as an extra payment—and I still owed June's $430. Suddenly I was responsible for rent ($775), utilities, a credit card bill, and another full car payment—just one month into the loan.

I had done everything "right." Paid early. Budgeted responsibly. But the system didn't care. By the end of the month, I had less than $10 in my checking account.

It never happened again.

From that moment forward, I began meticulously tracking my spending. I categorized every expense. I timed my savings transfers. My bank allowed six withdrawals from savings per month—and I assigned five of those to my most important bills. I didn't just become better at budgeting. I became obsessed with understanding my money.

Because I had to be. Even when I wasn't actively spending, the costs were still moving. If I didn't see them clearly, they were going to wreck me again.

From Survival to Strategy

The first version of my budget spreadsheet had seven tabs. It was messy, chaotic, and full of formulas, projections, and "what-if" scenarios. It was built for one person—me. It was a bunker I built in a financial storm. Every tab was a different angle of my money: car payments, hypothetical models, compounding debt, pension assumptions. I didn't share it. I didn't even think about who else might use it.

The newer version? One tab. Clean. Focused. Built to help anyone.

I stripped it down to only what mattered—because I realized people don't need complicated spreadsheets. They need clarity. They need tools that make sense the second they open them. They need something they'll actually use.

So I built a tool for them.

The shift was powerful. I moved from survival to strategy. From personal chaos to public clarity. From asking, "How do I get through the month?" to "How do I help others feel in control every day?"

That's what this book is about. The real, sometimes messy process of figuring out money—and building a life where it doesn't control you anymore.

One Last Thing…

If you picked up this book hoping I'd tell you how to save money, I'll be honest—this isn't that kind of book. Except for this one thing: if you're still renting your cable modem, you're getting fleeced.

Most providers charge $10 to $15 per month to rent a device that costs between $70 and $120 outright. Over two years, that's up to $360 for something worth $120. You're paying two to three times more just to let it sit quietly on your bill.

Congress won't help you, so I will—buy your own modem. You'll thank me later.

That's the kind of clarity I want to give you.

I'm not here to preach—I'm here to guide. To show you what worked for me, and what might work for you. You deserve dignity and control when it comes to your money. So let's stop judging ourselves for what we weren't taught, and start building the life we actually want.

Bridge From the Political to the Personal

Before we dive in, I want to be clear about who this book is for.

If you make less than $500,000 a year, this is your book. That number isn't arbitrary. In the 1940s, FDR proposed a 100% tax on income over $25,000 a year—the equivalent of about half a million today. His top marginal tax rate eventually hit 94%, because we understood something back then that we've forgotten now: concentrated wealth is a threat to democracy.

I believe the same logic still holds. If you're under that line, the system isn't working for you. You're not just surviving in a rigged economy—you're working for a millionaire and billionaire class you'll never be allowed to join.
If you're holding more than $10 million in assets? Then yes—I believe you should be taxed at 5%, maybe even 10% annually. Not to punish success, but to repair the damage. That money should be used to fund public education, rebuild infrastructure, support universal healthcare, and pay down the debt this system created.

People view socialism as a redistribution of wealth. I view it as a redistribution of theft—because for decades, we've handed trillions to the richest Americans while telling everyone else to budget harder.

A functioning country doesn't need billionaires. It needs shared stability. Until we get that back, we need new rules—and sharper tools.

That's the system. But this book isn't just about the system.

It's about how you survive inside it. How you plan your week, manage your bills, navigate debt, understand healthcare, negotiate with a partner, avoid traps, ask for help, and—yes—get your dignity back.

These are the short-term, medium-term, and long-term tools I wish someone had handed me sooner. They're not about chasing wealth. They're about reclaiming control.

Because when the rules are rigged, the only way forward is to get clear—and get smarter. Starting today.
Let's get into it.

The 5 Principles of Spending

Read this before you go any further.

Before we dive into numbers, categories, subscriptions, or any of the big-ticket traps, we need to get something clear.

This isn't just a budgeting book. It's a book about how to see the system for what it really is… and how to live freely inside it.

So let's start there—with five principles that shape everything you're about to read. You don't need to memorize them. You'll feel them. They'll show up in every chapter, every story, every shift in thinking. This is your new foundation.

1. You Spend Money Every Day—Even When You Do Nothing

This is the one I come back to more than any other.

Whether you leave your house or not, whether you work or not, whether you even wake up on time—your money is moving.

Rent. Insurance. Subscriptions. Interest. Electricity. That gym membership you forgot to cancel. These things don't pause because you behaved.

But here's the kicker: interest moves too.
If you owe money? It's growing.
If you've saved money? It's growing too.

That's the real lever: your money compounds—every day.
The only question is: for whom?
If your money is sitting in a savings account—earning even 4%—you're making quiet progress while you sleep.
If you're carrying debt at 20%, you're losing ground just as fast. You don't need to swipe your card for the cost to pile up. The system will do that for you.

Most people only think they're spending when they swipe. But you've already spent money before you roll out of bed—and you've either lost more to interest… or gained a little because you paid yourself first.

That's why I teach people to track their daily burn rate—because there's a cost to simply existing. Once you know your daily active spend—the leftover amount you truly control—everything changes. If your number is $25/day, that's it. That's your North Star. Spend $40 today? Tomorrow drops to $10. Spend $18 today? Bank the extra $7 instead of rolling it forward as "fun money." It's not about perfection—it's about balance. That daily active spend becomes your anchor. Your financial autopilot. The thing that keeps you from drifting without having to rewrite your budget every week.

Because here's the truth—there's also a cost to ignoring the math.

Every day you carry a balance, it gets heavier.
Every day you save, the future gets a little lighter.
That's the compound truth no one teaches early enough.

You don't need to understand Wall Street. You just need to know which way the current is flowing—and whether your money is working for you, or against you.

2. The System Is Designed to Make You Overspend

This isn't you being bad with money. This is a system that profits when you forget, delay, panic, or stay distracted.

It's not just designed to make you overspend—it's designed to extract. A little from your account, a little from your time, and a lot from your peace of mind.

Corporations make billions from auto-renewals. Banks profit from late fees. "Buy Now Pay Later" doesn't exist to help you—

it exists to stretch your budget just far enough that you don't notice the damage until it's too late.

While you're juggling bills and Googling interest rates, the real money is moving quietly—through stock buybacks, tax cuts, and loopholes the rest of us never get access to.
Here's the other trick: the system never encourages you to ask for help. Not from your government. Not from your community. Not even from a friend. Shame keeps you quiet. Complexity keeps you confused. And both keep the money flowing away from you.

This isn't a conspiracy theory. It's just capitalism without brakes. You're not broken. The system is working exactly as intended.

3. Big Purchases Shape Your Financial Future

A $5 coffee won't bankrupt you. A $50,000 mistake might.

Most personal finance advice focuses on small stuff—canceling subscriptions, skipping takeout, avoiding "frivolous" spending. But that's not where people fall behind.

They fall behind when they take on a mortgage they didn't fully understand… a student loan they thought was a golden ticket… or a car they "deserved" but couldn't actually afford to keep.

If it takes more than a month to pay off, it deserves more than a moment of thought.
Because these aren't just purchases. They're commitments.
Some of them will go on to shape the next ten years of your life.

4. Needing Less Is the Ultimate Financial Power

This one's emotional. But it's real.

Most of us are taught that money equals freedom. But that's only half true. Because the real secret—the one the system doesn't want you to hear—is that needing less gives you power faster than earning more ever will.

You don't have to move to the woods. You don't have to live like a monk. But the less you rely on debt, the less you chase validation through your spending, the freer you become.

Want real control? Stop trying to impress people who aren't paying your bills. Stop building your identity around what you can buy. Start building it around what you don't need anymore.

Here's the part no one tells you: when you need less, you also have more to give. Your time, your energy, even a little bit of your money. That's how community strength multiplies— through people who've freed themselves from chasing every dollar and can afford to show up for others.

5. Your Government Can Make Life Easier—If You Demand It

This might be the one people skip over. Don't.

Because the truth is, most of your personal financial stress isn't personal—it's structural. Germany has higher taxes than the U.S., but more disposable income. Why? Because they don't spend $1,000 a month on insurance, student loans, and childcare. Public money buys public stability. Here, we hand it to billionaires and then argue over crumbs.

But it's not just government. Community matters too. When you ask a neighbor for help, share costs with friends, or lean on local resources, you're not failing—you're participating in the oldest financial safety net humans ever built: each other. It only works if you're willing to do the same when someone else needs it.

That's how strength builds: not only by demanding better policy from the top, but also by showing up for each other at the ground level. Watching someone's kids. Driving them to the doctor. Splitting rent or food costs. Volunteering your time. Paying it forward when you're able.

Every time the news explodes over guns or bathrooms or book bans, ask yourself what just got passed in the tax code. Ask yourself what billionaires bought while the rest of us were yelling. Remember: real financial stability is collective. It comes from strengthening the systems around you—through policy, through accountability, and through communities that give back as much as they receive.

You deserve more than budgeting tips. You deserve a government that works for you and a community that refuses to leave you behind. Neither happens by accident. Both only exist if we fight for them, invest in them, and strengthen them—day by day.

These five principles are the spine of this book. They're the filter. The compass. The why.

You'll hear them again, in different ways. You'll see them play out in stories, in examples, in strategies. But you'll feel them most when something clicks. When a new idea settles into your gut and you think:

"Why didn't anyone teach me this sooner?"

That's when the work begins. Because you can't rewrite your financial story until someone finally hands you the first page.

Chapter 1: The Cost of Doing Nothing

You don't need to mess up to fall behind financially. You don't need to buy the wrong car, go on a shopping spree, or skip work.
All you have to do… is exist.

Every hour has a price—even the quiet ones.
Every day takes a bite out of your bank account, even if you never leave the house. That's the hidden truth of American money: we're leaking, not spending. Unless you spot the drip, you're already sinking.

I don't write this book from a place of hypothesis—I write from the trenches. I've worked jobs, managed budgets, run scenarios. I've seen what happens when good people with decent incomes still end up stressed, behind, or out of options.

Not because they're lazy.
Not because they're irresponsible.
But because the system is quiet in how it steals from you.

Money isn't just a tool. It's a current that never stops. Whether you're clocked in or not, whether you're working two jobs or healing from burnout, money is moving. Because if you're not tracking it, you're not in control of it.

Time is money. But so is rest.
So is caregiving. So is unemployment. So is recovery.
There's a cost to simply existing—and that's the first thing no one tells you.

Most people only think about money when they swipe their card.
Groceries, gas, drinks with friends—that's when we feel the cost. But the real danger isn't what you spend when you're paying attention. It's what disappears when you aren't.

That's what I call passive spending—money that leaks out quietly, invisibly, just to maintain the life you already have. Rent, bills, subscriptions, debt payments, interest charges, fees. It's the background noise of your financial life... until it becomes a roar.

Let me give you a real-life example.

Back in 2019—before the pandemic turned remote work into a coastal migration—I was taking a rideshare home from work in San Diego. My old Volkswagen had finally become too expensive to keep running, so I sold it off and relied on other options.

My driver that day was friendly. He told me about his new apartment. He and his girlfriend had just moved in. "Only $3,000 a month," he said with a big smile.

He was working two jobs—rideshare and an Amazon warehouse. I respected the grind. But I also couldn't let the math slide.
"Do you realize you need to make $100 a day after taxes just to cover rent?" I asked.

He blinked. He hadn't thought of it that way.

Let's do the breakdown:

- $3,000 ÷ 30 days = $100/day
- That's just rent. No groceries, no gas, no internet, no insurance. Just the roof.

At $16–17/hour—which is what a lot of rideshare and warehouse workers earn—he was working full-time just to hold his spot in the system. That's not luxury. That's survival.

What struck me wasn't that he was irresponsible. It was that no one had ever helped him see his daily cost of living. Not his school. Not his job. Not even his bank. Certainly not the apps or companies he worked for.

He didn't need budgeting advice.
He needed someone to show him how the math really worked.

That's the truth for a lot of us—most people don't need shaming. They need clarity. Sometimes they need community to help them see what the system won't teach.

That's when it hit me. This system doesn't crash most people— it just wears them down. Slowly, invisibly, through passive spending they never agreed to… and never questioned.

That's not living.
That's treading water.

That moment hit me. I realized just how differently I viewed money. I also realized that this guy, like so many others, was stuck in a system that never taught him how to think about money daily.

The Myth of No-Spend Days

We love the illusion of a "good money day."
No takeout, no online shopping, no Target run. No temptation won.
"Look at me," we think. "I didn't spend a dime."
But that's the lie.
Because you did spend—you just didn't swipe.

There's no such thing as a no-spend day.

Your rent didn't hit pause.
Your car insurance didn't take the day off.
Your phone plan didn't pat you on the back and say, "Nice job."

You still paid to exist. The charges were just invisible.

Here's what a typical passive spend might look like:

- Rent: $2,100/month → $70/day
- Internet: $60/month → $2/day
- Streaming services: $45/month → $1.50/day
- Phone: $100/month → $3.33/day
- Car insurance: $180/month → $6/day
- Health insurance: $450/month → $15/day
- Subscriptions you forgot about: ???

That's not even counting food, gas, child care, or student loans.

You could literally sleep in all day, never touch your keys or your wallet, and still burn through nearly $100 just for being alive.

Now zoom out: that's $700 a week, or over $36,000 a year—before you've actively chosen a single thing.

This is why financial stress shows up even when you're "being good."
Because the cost of doing nothing is still a cost.
When you don't see that daily drip, you can't manage it.
You're not budgeting—you're reacting.
Usually, you're just reacting to overdrafts.

Death by Auto-Charge

There's a pattern I see all the time. People cut the obvious stuff… no happy hours, no Sunday brunch, no late-night takeout… then wonder why the account balance barely moves.

The quiet leak is hiding in plain sight: premium delivery memberships, a stack of streaming services, a meditation app from years ago, a fitness subscription on pause. Nothing outrageous on its own. Together… a steady drip.

Open your phone's subscriptions page and your bank or card statements. You probably won't want to... do it anyway. Many people find $50–$200 a month they've stopped using. That's $600–$2,400 a year. Not on joy, not on emergencies, not on your future. Just... auto-charges.

Here's the trap: you did the hard part — you stopped spending actively. But the fire keeps burning underneath because the fuel line is still open.

Passive spending hides in the background. If you're not hunting for it, it keeps draining you while you're out there trying to be "responsible."

The Trial Trap Rule

Subscriptions aren't just a service model.
They're a trapdoor—especially the ones that start with "free."

Whether it's a 7-day, 30-day, or "first month on us" offer, the real business model isn't generosity. It's forgetfulness. These companies aren't hoping you love the service—they're hoping you forget to cancel.

So here's my rule, and I stick to it religiously:

Cancel the day you sign up.
Not the day before it renews.
Not when your trial is about to end.
The day you start.

Why? Because you've already unlocked the free period.
Canceling doesn't take it away. It just prevents future charges.

Here's my three-step system:

- Cancel immediately.
- Set a calendar reminder for the trial's end.
- Only sign up if you'd pay full price anyway.

That last one matters. If you wouldn't pay for it later, don't convince yourself it's "free" now.

Because it's not free. It's delayed.
Most people don't forget because they're lazy.
They forget because the system is built that way.
It's called sludge—and it's a business strategy.

We'll dig deeper into that sludge in Chapter 17. For now, just know: the system doesn't profit when you're mindful. It profits when you're on autopilot.

It's counting on it.

A New Way to See Your Budget

Here's the truth: every time the clock strikes midnight, your money moves—even if you don't.

There's a cost to today. There's a cost to tomorrow. And there was a cost to yesterday, whether you remember what you spent or not.

Whether you own, rent, or live with family… whether you're single, partnered, or raising three kids… every day has a financial footprint. Your rent is ticking upward by the hour. Your phone plan is charging you for notifications you ignored. Your internet bill doesn't care if you worked from home or not.

It's happening every day. Most of us don't track it—not because we're irresponsible, but because we were never taught to think about money this way.

This is why I keep bringing up passive spending. It's the part of your budget that just... bleeds. Slowly. Silently. Predictably. But when you start minimizing it? You start gaining power.

Power to redirect your money. Power to plan for what matters. Power to feel some breathing room again.

Here's what most people do: they split their expenses by paycheck. Rent comes from one. Everything else comes from the other. It kind of works—until it doesn't.

Because that second paycheck? It has to cover groceries. Social plans. Gas. Medicine. Travel. Birthday gifts. Unexpected bills. Emergencies.

That's how we fall behind. Not from irresponsibility—but from invisibility. From not having a clear sense of how much each day actually costs. From treating money as a monthly concept while living in a daily reality.

Worst case? You miss out on something you really wanted. Not because it was too expensive—but because you didn't plan for it.

It doesn't have to be like that.

Your Challenge: Find Your Burn Rate

Here's where the awareness becomes action.

Start by writing down every fixed cost you have.
Rent. Insurance. Phone. Internet. Gym. Subscriptions. Debt payments. Anything that comes out monthly whether you're ready or not.

Add it all up.
Then divide that number by 30.

That's your daily passive spend.
That's what it costs you just to exist.

Not to grow. Not to thrive. Not to enjoy your life.
Just to wake up.
Now ask yourself two things:

1. Is this where I want my money to go?
2. Is this who I want to be paying every day?

If you feel even a little uncomfortable with the answers, good.
That discomfort isn't shame—it's clarity. It means your brain is
waking up to something you weren't taught but always
deserved to know.

When you see your burn rate, you can plan around it.
When you reduce your passive costs, you free up your future.
When you know your number, you stop drifting.
Once you minimize the cost of doing nothing…

You free yourself to start doing something.

Chapter 2: The Daily Spend Mindset

People like to spend where they want to be—not where they are.

We dress for the job we want. We decorate our homes for the lifestyle we imagine. We buy the car we think matches our future, not our current income.

But here's the question:
Is that car something you truly can't afford…
or is it just making your daily life harder so you can feel a little fancier?

If the answer is "both," then you're probably overspending, stressed, and overdue for a mindset shift.

Let me be clear—this isn't a sermon about being frugal. I'm not here to push scarcity. I'm not anti-latte or anti-vacation or anti-nice things.

I'm anti-spending that steals from your future.

My goal is simple: I want you to spend in a way that makes your life better—not just today, but a week from now… a month from now… even years from now.

That starts with something no one ever taught us:

Your budget isn't just about the numbers in it.
It's about how you approach those numbers.
This is where it gets weird. I'm going to talk about budgets—but how much you make? That's the last thing I want to focus on.

A Calorie-Based Wake-Up Call

Let me try a comparison that helped me rethink everything.

Think about calories. Most adults need somewhere between 2,000 and 3,000 per day, depending on size, activity level, and health goals. It's a daily rhythm—intake, output, balance.

Now imagine I said, "You've got 90,000 calories to use this month."
You'd be overwhelmed. You wouldn't know where to start. You'd have no instinct for pacing. You'd probably under-eat one day, overeat the next, and lose all sense of what's actually working.

But that's exactly how most people approach money.

They get a paycheck—maybe once, twice, or even three times a month—and they try to mentally stretch it across time. Sometimes 14 days. Sometimes 31. Maybe longer if they're hoping to roll leftovers into next month. But they don't know their number per day.

Here's the problem: we don't live in months.
We live in days. We wake up, we eat, we commute, we work, we rest, we scroll. Every day has a rhythm, a routine, a cost.

So why are we managing our money like we're operating on a monthly timeline…
when emotionally, practically, and behaviorally, we spend in daily cycles?

We need short-term thinking to hit our long-term goals.

We need a daily lens.
Because let's face it: even if you make a lot of money, most people don't feel financially secure. A big reason is that we try

to manage money in time blocks we don't emotionally live in.
We wake up in days—not months.

When I talk about budgeting, I don't start by asking how much
you make.
I ask how you spend.

Because here's the uncomfortable truth:
Income doesn't solve financial stress.
There are people making $40,000 who feel free and in control.
And there are people making $140,000 who feel broke every
single day.

Why? Because most of us have been trained to focus on the
wrong metric.

We obsess over how much we earn.
We chase raises, promotions, titles.
We glorify the hustle and shame the slowdown.
Meanwhile, in the process, we ignore the one thing that actually
shapes our day-to-day experience: spending behavior.

The system is built to push earnings over awareness.
But real freedom doesn't come from earning more—it comes
from needing less.

This is why I don't care about your income—not at first.
Because if you spend more than you bring in, it doesn't matter
whether you make $35K or $350K—you're still running behind.

It's not about how much we make.
It's about how we spend.

The Danger of Lifestyle Creep

Let's talk about the invisible upgrade that wrecks most budgets.

You get a raise.
You celebrate a little—you've earned it.
You order takeout more often.
You swap your $10 gym for the boutique studio with eucalyptus towels.
You move into a nicer apartment because, hey, you make more now.

Fast-forward six months:
You're making more money, but you feel just as stressed.
You're working harder, but you're not getting ahead.
You're still saying no to things you care about... because the money's already gone.

What happened?

Lifestyle creep.
The slow, subtle inflation of your daily life.
It doesn't happen all at once—it slips in under the radar.
And before you know it, your new income isn't creating breathing room—it's just feeding new habits.

Lifestyle Creep Is a Liar

Lifestyle creep always says the same thing:
"You deserve this."

You worked hard. You survived the burnout. You made it through the layoff.
Why not upgrade the car? Try the restaurant? Get the nicer apartment?

Honestly? Sometimes you should.
But the problem is: it never stops there.

Because lifestyle creep isn't about joy. It's about baseline.

You don't feel happier. You feel normal—but now normal costs more.

And once your spending becomes your identity, cutting back doesn't feel like progress.
It feels like failure.

That's the trap.

Freedom doesn't come from spending more.
It comes from needing less.

From Education to Awareness

At the end of this chapter, I'll share a spreadsheet I built to help you see your expenses through a daily lens. But before we get there, let me show you how this mindset started for me.

I've made more than the median income for most of my adult life. I earned a marketing degree from Syracuse University, then went on to get my MBA from UCLA Anderson. Statistically, a college degree adds about $1 million in lifetime earnings compared to a high school diploma.

So yeah—I came into adulthood with some financial advantages.

But none of that taught me how to budget.

Not one class. Not one job. Not even business school.
That's the story for a lot of people, regardless of background or degree. You can earn more, but if you don't know how to track or pace your spending, it slips through your fingers just the same.

I had to build my system from the ground up...

Starting with a car payment.

The Volkswagen That Changed My Mindset

Remember that Volkswagen I mentioned in Chapter 1? The one I finally ditched because it became too expensive to maintain?

That car was my financial wake-up call.

The payment was $430 a month. Not astronomical—but at the time, it felt huge. I was getting paid every two weeks, but some months had a third check, depending on the calendar.

So I came up with a system:
I'd always keep at least $215 in my account. That was half the payment. If I had that, then no matter when the bill hit, I'd be ready.
It worked.

That little change gave me more peace of mind than any budgeting app or "spend less" advice ever had. For the first time, I was preparing for a future expense instead of reacting to it.
Once I got that habit down, I applied it to rent—my biggest expense. At the time, I was lucky to have sub-$1,000 rent in San Diego, so I split it the same way: $500 per paycheck. No stress. No scramble.

That meant I was now setting aside $715 from every check, just to cover those two fixed expenses.

At the time, my paycheck was about $1,400.

If I was setting aside $715 for rent and the car payment, that left me with $685 per pay period. And instead of treating that as one big lump sum, I broke it down.

How much was that per day until the next check?

That one shift changed everything.

The Birth of the Daily Spend Mindset

I took the leftover $685 and divided it across the number of days in the pay period. Sometimes that was 14 days, sometimes a little more depending on the month.

Turns out, I had around $49 a day for everything else.
Gas. Food. Fun. Errands. Social stuff. Emergencies.

That $49 wasn't some strict allowance—it was a lens. A pulse check. It gave me rhythm. It helped me stay grounded in the present while planning for the future.
Most importantly?
It gave me control over time.

Here's how I used it—starting on day one of a new pay period:

Option A: Stay Strict
If I spent $30 on gas, I had $19 left for the day. I stayed within my $49 and called it a win. If I came in under, I moved the leftover to savings and called it "spent." That made saving feel like an intentional choice—not a sacrifice.

Option B: The Savings Reward
If I spent $30 on gas—a necessity—I treated it as semi-passive. My "everything-else" budget actually nudged up a bit. That $19 in unspent cash spread out over the next 13 days, raising my daily rate from $49 to $50.

Option C: The Impulse Penalty
If I spent $30 on gas and then walked inside Costco and dropped $55 inside (because Costco) plus $5 on the hot dog combo and friends, that $90 total hit hard. With 13 days left, that extra $60 overage dropped my daily rate by about $5—from $49 to $44.

Either way, I had a system. A rhythm. A daily guide. For the first time, I felt ahead of my money instead of behind it.

And the weird part? It felt better than any raise I'd ever gotten. I wasn't making more. I was just seeing clearly.

Your number might not be $49—it might be $25, or $60, or $12. The dollar figure doesn't matter. What matters is that once you know it, that number becomes your baseline. Spend $40 on a $25/day budget? Tomorrow drops to $10. Come in under budget? Bank the extra immediately. The math is simple—but the behavior is what changes everything.

Because once you start seeing your money in daily rhythm, it stops controlling you.
You stop reacting.
You start pacing.
And pacing—not perfection—is how real control begins.

Once you start thinking in daily rhythm, you'll notice every windfall feels different.
A bonus, a tax refund, even an extra paycheck in the calendar—suddenly you see it for what it really is: not a jackpot, but a moment to breathe.

The 3-Paycheck Trap

Every so often, the calendar gifts you a little bonus:
Three paychecks in one month instead of two.

It feels like winning the lottery.

But here's the trap:
Your expenses didn't change.
Your rent is still due once.
Your phone bill still comes monthly.
Your streaming services are still creeping along in the background.

So what happens?

That extra check feels like "fun money"—and you spend it like it's free. But within days, it's gone. And next month? You're right back where you started.

That third paycheck isn't a gift.
It's a tool.

Use it to:

- Pay off debt
- Pad your emergency fund
- Pre-pay next month's passive costs
- Build momentum toward something bigger

Don't treat it like extra.
Treat it like leverage.

Because in a system that rarely gives you room to breathe, a third paycheck isn't a bonus—it's breathing room. And how you use it can shift everything.
That's how you turn a calendar fluke… into financial momentum.

The Spreadsheet That Changed Everything

Now it's your turn to see your money clearly.

I built a spreadsheet that made all of this click—the same one I still use today.
And yes—this exact spreadsheet is free. You'll find the link at the end of the next chapter, so don't go building your own yet.

It's simple, not flashy—but it changed the way I understand my own finances.

Here's how it works:

Step 1: Enter your fixed monthly expenses.
Rent. Car payment. Phone. Insurance. Subscriptions.
This is your passive spend—what you owe whether you leave
your house or not.

Step 2: Divide that number by 30.
That gives you your daily passive spend. The cost of doing
nothing.

Step 3: Estimate your variable expenses.
Groceries. Gas. Coffee. Gym drop-ins. This is your active spend
—the money you control day to day.

Step 4: Compare it all to your take-home pay.
Does the math work?

If your daily budget comes out negative, that's not a failure.
It's a starting point.

It means your system is out of alignment—not that you are.

This isn't about shame. It's about information.
Because you can't fix what you can't see.
Spoiler alert: for most people, passive spending is the problem.
It's not the $6 coffee or the shoes on sale—it's the $2,300 rent,
the auto-renewing bills, the quiet drip of commitments that steal
your options before the month even begins.

The biggest drip?
The one that drowns most people?

It's housing.

We'll tackle how to fix that in the next few chapters. But for
now, know this:

Passive expenses are usually the biggest culprits. Housing is almost always the heavyweight.
We'll dig into that more soon.

But this is where we begin: with the daily spend mindset.

The Leftover Rule

Here's one last habit that changed everything for me—and it's dead simple:

At the end of each pay period, if I had any money left from my daily spend budget, I didn't leave it sitting there.

I moved it.

Into savings.
Toward my highest-interest debt.
Into a retirement account.
Sometimes even into a travel fund.

I didn't wait for a perfect moment. I didn't tell myself I'd do it next week.
I just moved the leftovers—automatically.

Because leftovers aren't a reward.
They're building blocks.

They're the bricks that form your safety net. The fuel for your freedom. The quiet compounding force that makes you stronger with every paycheck.

You don't need a financial windfall to get ahead.
You need a repeatable habit that keeps stacking.

Once you start stacking…
you'd be amazed how fast the wall goes up.

That wall you're building—brick by brick—isn't just made of daily discipline. It's made of understanding where your money moves passively and where you actively direct it. Next, we'll break down that difference and show you how to turn both into tools that work for you.

The stronger your wall gets, the more you'll be able to lend bricks to someone else—to support a friend, a family member, or even your broader community when they need it.

Chapter 3: Passive vs. Active Spend

O kay—we've mapped out your expenses. You've stared down your burn rate. You've seen how much of your money vanishes before you even get a chance to touch it.

It's kind of like cleaning out a cluttered closet. You pull everything out and realize you've been paying for things you don't use, don't need, or forgot you even owned.

That was your passive spending—the money that moves whether you do or not. Rent. Insurance. Subscriptions. Bills. Auto-payments. It's the financial background noise of your life.

Now here comes the empowering part:
Looking at what's left.

That leftover space?
That's your active spending.

That's where your freedom lives.

The goal isn't to be perfect. It's to be intentional. This is the moment where you start managing your money instead of reacting to it.

What Are Passive and Active Spending?

Let's break it down clearly.

Some books or budgeting apps will call these "fixed vs. variable" or "committed vs. discretionary" expenses.

But I use different language for a reason—because those terms are clinical. Spreadsheet terms. They miss the emotional reality of how money works in real life.

Here's how I define it:

- Passive Spend = the money you pay just to maintain your life.
  Rent. Insurance. Subscriptions. Loan payments. Phone.
  Internet. Utilities. Savings. Investments. It's fixed or semi-
  fixed—and it happens whether you engage with it or not.
- Active Spend = the money you spend when you're in control.
  Groceries. Gas. Clothes. Restaurants. Gifts. Coffee. Travel.
  Impulse buys. This is where decisions happen in real time.

Here's the key:

Passive spending is mostly locked in.
Active spending is flexible.

Active spending feels like the only place we can cut, so most
people obsess over it. We guilt ourselves over groceries. We
cancel date nights. We second-guess a $7 smoothie.
If your passive expenses are eating up 80–90% of your
paycheck, you could live like a monk and still feel broke.

That's the trap. Now that you see it, you can start flipping the
script. Ironically, it's the passive spending that often controls the
whole equation.

Let's say you make $4,000 a month after taxes.

If your passive spending—rent, insurance, subscriptions, loan
payments—adds up to $3,200, that leaves you with $800.

Not for saving.
Not for investing.
Not for building a future.

That $800 is for everything else: groceries, gas, social plans,
clothes, emergencies, birthdays, parking tickets, impulse Target
runs, surprise vet bills, coffee, fun.

Most people don't do that math.

They see the $4,000 paycheck and assume they have $4,000 to spend.
Then they wonder why the card balance creeps up.
Why their checking account empties three days before payday.
Why they feel anxious swiping a card—even for essentials.

This is the moment a lot of people say, "I'm just bad with money."

But the truth is, they're not bad with money.
They're just not looking at how much of their income is already spoken for before they even start living their life.

Are You Overspending or Just Overcommitted?

A lot of people blame themselves when the money doesn't stretch.

"I must be overspending."
"I need to stop eating out."
"I shouldn't have bought that hoodie."
"I'm just bad at budgeting."

But pause for a second.
Ask yourself this:

Is your budget actually broken… or is it just overloaded?

If 80–90% of your income disappears into fixed costs the moment your paycheck hits, you don't have a spending problem.
You have a space problem.

It's like trying to eat healthy on 100 calories a day.
Even one mistake throws everything off. And the stress of trying to stay "perfect" becomes its own punishment.

You're not failing.
You're trying to breathe inside a system that gives you no air.

You're not bad at budgeting.
You're just playing a rigged game.

Let's fix that.

The Balance Scale

Picture one of those old-fashioned justice scales—two pans, one on each side.

On one side: your passive spend.
On the other: your active spend.

If your passive spend is too heavy, the scale tips—and you're stuck.
You're not thriving. You're maintaining. You're surviving.

If your active spend is oversized, you might be having fun—but you're not saving, investing, or preparing for what's next.

The goal isn't to make both sides equal.
The goal is balance—whatever that looks like for your life.

You want:

- Enough passive spend to cover what keeps your life stable
- Enough active spend to give you choice, joy, and flexibility
- Plus a little margin for the future—because future you deserves stability too

If that balance isn't there yet? That's okay. The next step is to shrink what you can't control in the moment—your passive spend—so you can expand what you can: your active spend.

That's where momentum begins.

Organizing Your Passive Spend

This is where most of the "work" happens—but it's also where you get the most immediate wins.

Passive expenses are your predictable leaks.
They happen whether you leave the house or not, whether you swipe a card or not, whether you're paying attention or not.

That makes them powerful—because they're also the easiest to clean up.

Start small. List your passive expenses from smallest to largest. It's often easier to trim five $20 charges than one $500 one.

Some examples:

- Cancel the streaming service you binged last winter and forgot about
- Cut the gym you never go to (no shame—your walk counts)
- Downgrade your phone plan or shop for a new provider

These are low-emotion cuts. You make the decision once, and the savings repeat.

That's the beauty of passive cuts: they don't rely on willpower. You cancel once, and the savings show up every month.

Passive Doesn't Mean Wasteful

When people hear "passive spending," they assume it's all bad. That it's money leaking out without benefit. But there's one passive expense that actually builds your future—and that's saving.

Yes, saving is a passive spend. It's money you remove from circulation today. It doesn't get you coffee. It doesn't get you a trip. It just sits there… until one day it saves you.

That's the point. You're spending forward. You're locking in stability you haven't needed yet—but will.

This is why I don't believe in "saving whatever's left." That's how most people treat it—and most people end up saving nothing. Because there's always something else to spend on.

Saving isn't what you do after you budget. It's what makes the budget work.

That's why I call it a positive passive. It's the only kind of money that exits your checking account without regret. You don't miss it—because it's still yours. It just moved from your "right now" to your "someday."

Because here's the truth most budget books skip:
Saving is spending. You're just buying your future in advance. Same with investing—it's delayed spending with a better return.

If you want to make this effortless, you don't wait until the end of the month. You don't cross your fingers hoping there's money left to save. You automate it.

Sweeping Savings into the Shadows

Here's the trick to building savings that actually stick: treat it like spending.

Not like an afterthought. Not like a leftover. Not like something you'll get to if the month goes smoothly. That's a recipe for nothing. If your savings plan depends on what's left over, you're telling your future self they only get what's spared—not what's prioritized.

Savings should leave your account the moment your paycheck arrives—automatically, without hesitation. No decisions. No second-guessing. Just one less thing to manage.

Keep it simple to start:

If you automatically move $42 from every paycheck—and you're paid every 14 days—that's $3 a day quietly leaving your active spending.

What does that actually do?

- In a single month, that's about $84 you've set aside without trying.
- In a year, that's $1,092—before you've earned a single penny of interest.

That's one small habit—one quiet decision—building a thousand-dollar buffer in a year without feeling like sacrifice. That's just an example. Maybe you can do $5 a day instead—that's $70 every paycheck, over $1,800 a year. Or $10 a day if you're in a stronger position—over $3,600 a year, untouched, quietly growing in the background.
You don't have to pick the perfect number right now. You just have to start with something that doesn't break your daily budget. The amount matters less than building the system that moves money away from temptation automatically.

Where does it go? That's up to you:
A high-yield savings account. A rainy-day fund. A future trip. A down payment. An emergency you'll no longer need to throw on a credit card.

Saving isn't something you do if there's anything left. It's the first move. The quiet, automatic act of paying yourself forward.

You're not reducing your lifestyle—you're buying freedom one paycheck at a time. That freedom doesn't just stay with you—it ripples. The less trapped you are, the more present you can be for your family, your community, and causes bigger than yourself. With each transfer, each quiet deposit, you're building a version of yourself that feels less pressure and more control.

Let's talk about the "20% rule" for active spending

Here's a useful benchmark to gut-check your numbers:

Try to keep your active spending at or under 20–35% of your take-home pay.

Why that range?

Because your active spend covers everything you actually feel:

- Groceries
- Gas (Do you ride it until E? That's an active choice.)
- Gifts
- Fun
- Emergencies
- Coffee, cravings, and chaos

This is your choice space—the part of your budget where you still get to say yes or no.

If that space is too tight, every little decision starts to feel stressful. You're second-guessing groceries. Resenting birthdays. Canceling plans you actually care about.

If your active spend is under 10%? That's not discipline—it's usually a red flag.

It probably means your passive spending is too high, and you're suffocating under fixed costs.
The solution isn't to tighten your grip even more.
It's not to cut out the $6 coffee.
It's to look upstream.

Because if there's no air in your budget, you don't need to
hustle harder.
You need to restructure.

Building Your Active Budget

Once you've calculated your passive spending, subtract it from
your monthly income.
What you have left is your active budget—the money you
actually get to work with.

Now divide that number by 30.
That's your daily active spend—the amount you can use each
day on anything outside your fixed obligations.

Let's run a simple example:

- Monthly income: $4,000
- Passive spend: $3,200
- Remaining: $800
- Daily active spend: $800 ÷ 30 = $26.67/day

That $26.67 is for everything else.
Food. Gas. Gifts. Hobbies. Surprises. Joy.

It's not a huge amount. And if you don't plan it, it slips through
your fingers fast.
So here's what I do:

I pre-assign some of my active budget to the semi-fixed stuff.

Let's say I know I usually spend $300/month on groceries.
That's $10/day.

So now I mentally reduce my active spend:
$26.67 − $10 = $16.67/day of flexible spending.
That helps me plan ahead instead of just reacting.

Saving for the Fun Stuff

Now let's take it a step further.

You've got a trip coming up in six months. It'll cost you $900.

Instead of panicking later or putting it on a credit card, break it down now:

- $900 ÷ 6 months = $150/month
- $150 ÷ 30 days = $5/day

So you reduce your daily active spend by $5/day and stash that money in a separate account or budget category.

If your original active spend was $26.67/day, now it's $21.67/day.
Simple. Clear. Intentional.

You don't have to change your whole life.
You don't need to cancel joy.

You just need to plan for it—one day at a time.

That $5/day doesn't feel like much. But it adds up fast.
When the time comes to book the flight, pay for the hotel, or buy that concert ticket?

It won't feel like a financial hit.
It'll feel like something you already earned.

You've just bought your future vacation one day at a time.

This is how you stretch your income without feeling broke. And it's how you build freedom without relying on major life changes like getting a new job or moving across the country.

What If the Math Doesn't Work?

Here's the part where reality might sting a little.

If your active spending number comes out negative, you've got a passive spending problem.

If your active spending number is tiny, you've still got a passive spending problem.

If your active spending number is large, but you're not saving, not investing, not making progress?

Then you don't have a spending problem—you have a clarity problem.

In all three cases, the answer is the same:
You've got work to do.

But here's the good news—that work is within your control.

It might take time.
It might require uncomfortable conversations, temporary trade-offs, or a shift in priorities.

But it doesn't require a new degree.
It doesn't require a second job.
It doesn't require permission.

It starts with awareness.
Then intention.
Then consistency.

It starts with awareness. Then intention. Then consistency.

Start Fresh, Every Time

Here's one habit that can completely change the way you save money:

At the end of your spending period—whether that's every two weeks, once a month, or whenever you get paid—take whatever's left in your active spend budget... and move it to savings.

Not part of it.
Not most of it.
All of it.

If you gave yourself $500 for two weeks and only spent $400, don't roll that extra $100 into the next cycle. Don't treat it like bonus money. Transfer it into savings or investments immediately—and then start fresh with the next paycheck.

Same amount. Same rules. Same plan.

Why? Because this does two things:

1. It keeps your lifestyle from creeping up just because you had a good week.
2. It turns saving into a habit, not a reaction.

Over time, this creates a self-contained rhythm. You're not budgeting based on vibes or leftovers. You're budgeting based on decisions. That's where the power comes from.

Know Your Numbers

Take five minutes—right now if you can—and do the math.

1. Write down your monthly income after taxes.
2. Add up all your passive expenses: rent, insurance, subscriptions, loan payments—everything that comes out on its own.
3. Subtract that number from your income.
4. Divide the leftover by 30.

That's your daily active spend—the amount you actually have control over.

If the number's too low, don't panic. That's why you're here.
If it's too high and you're not saving, that's a signal too.

If it lands somewhere in the middle? Great.
Now you've got a number you can build around.

Locking In Your Daily Active Spend

Here's where the numbers get real.

Once you've calculated your passive spend and landed on your daily active spend, you don't need a brand-new budget every week. You just need one fixed rule:

- One daily active spend target.
- One consistent habit.
- One truth: Overspending today means spending less tomorrow.

If your number is $25/day, that's it. That's your North Star. Every choice you make runs against it. Spend $40 today? Tomorrow drops to $10. Spend $18 today? You don't roll the extra $7 into more takeout—you move it into savings, pay down debt, or put it toward something future-you will thank you for.

This isn't about perfection—it's about balance. Some days run high, some run low. The key is adjusting in real time so the average holds.

That's how your daily active spend stops being just a calculation and starts being a habit—a simple, repeatable system that works quietly in the background, paycheck after paycheck.

If you want help running the numbers, I've built a free budgeting sheet you can use. Just go to **www.zackfields.com/budget**. On that page, you'll find a link to Google Sheets where you enter your income and expenses. The sheet then calculates two things for you: your passive spend per day (the red box) and your available active spend per day (the green box). That green box is your daily active spend — the part you can actually control. Make a copy for yourself, update it whenever your expenses change, and you'll always know exactly where you stand.

Because once you know your number...
you stop making excuses, and start making choices.

Do that long enough?
Your future looks a lot less like guesswork—
and a lot more like freedom.

That's exactly where we're headed next—straight into housing, the expense that quietly swallows most budgets. If passive spending is the leak, housing is usually the flood. Let's see how it happens and what you can do about it.

Chapter 4: Housing – The Heavyweight

There is nothing more fundamental, foundational, or fateful (yes, I love alliteration) than housing. It's the heavyweight of your budget—the one expense you carry whether you're awake or asleep, employed or between jobs.

If you haven't retired yet—and let's be real, even for many who have—housing is probably the single largest cost in your life. Unlike gas or groceries, it doesn't ebb and flow. It doesn't wait until you get paid. It just… shows up. Every single day.

That's why this category isn't just important—it's make-or-break. Housing isn't a monthly decision. It's a long-term anchor that shapes every other financial choice that you make. Yes, some people land a six-month sublet or move every year, but most of us? We stay. We re-sign. We settle in. Whether it's a 12-month lease or a 30-year mortgage, the gravity is the same.

Because here's the truth: most people don't move out the day their lease ends. Most don't sell their house the day the mortgage is paid off. Housing decisions linger. They stick. They shape not just where your money goes—but how your life unfolds.

I'll talk about renting vs. owning in a second. But let's agree on one goal upfront: housing costs should shrink as you age. Whether you rent forever or pay off a home completely, your long-term financial freedom depends on reducing this burden over time.

Maybe that means downsizing. Maybe it means living with someone. Maybe it means taking the road less glamorous. But if you can cut this single expense in half—or better yet, close to zero—you unlock a kind of freedom no raise or bonus can match.

Economists, Bias, and the Housing Myth

This is also the chapter where my love-hate relationship with economists kicks in—despite being one myself.

Economists are supposed to think in systems. But too often, they think in bubbles—ones built from privilege, proximity, or theory. Especially the PhDs. Many of them come from modest means and then—boom—they land a six-figure job in academia or policy. And that jump? It creates distance. Emotional, financial, and intellectual.

That same distance exists in the data, too. What I call *Economic Distance*—the gap between what previous generations could afford and what we can't—is one of the most under-measured forces in modern economics. We keep tracking home prices year over year like that tells the story. It doesn't. The real story is sixty years long—three generations of widening separation between wages and shelter. If we measured that distance instead of just motion, we'd see how far affordability has drifted and how policy decisions—tax cuts, deregulation, interest rate cycles—have slowly priced entire generations out of stability.

And when economists live inside that kind of privilege, they stop noticing the gap. They stop budgeting the same way. They're not racing to make rent at the end of the month. They forget what it feels like to juggle payments, split checks, or run grocery math in the cereal aisle. Instead, they default to averages and hypotheses that make clean sense on paper… and almost no sense in real life.

It's a proximity bias. They surround themselves with other financially secure thinkers—and their empathy gap grows.

I remember listening to Freakonomics Radio (Episode 518) when Yale economist James Choi said something that stopped me cold: he's a renter for life. He described buying a home as "prepaying rent," and said a rational person should be

indifferent between renting and owning. That kind of honesty?
Rare. And deeply comforting. Especially for Millennials and
Gen Z, who've been told since childhood that homeownership
is the only ticket to real wealth.

Contrast that with economists like Ed Glaeser from Harvard,
who appeared in Episode 566. He admitted that fixing
affordability could mean asking homeowners to accept a 30%
drop in their most important asset. But notice what's baked into
that statement: it assumes housing is supposed to be an asset in
the first place.

Why? Why should the roof over your head double as a stock
portfolio? Why should affordability mean "losing wealth"
rather than "gaining access"?

Plenty of countries reject that premise entirely. In Austria, about
60% of Vienna's residents live in publicly owned or subsidized
housing. The goal isn't appreciation—it's shelter. In Japan,
housing permits are issued at nearly ten times the rate of the
U.S., because the point isn't to guard property values… it's to
make sure people can actually live where they work.

But here in America, we've built a housing market that treats
stability as a threat. We've so financialized homes that
economists and politicians can't even imagine affordability
without framing it as a 30% loss. That's not objective analysis—
that's Stockholm syndrome dressed up as economics.

Because here's the thing: buying a home isn't like buying an
investment—it's like buying a car with a $1 million loan,
praying the dealership tells you it's worth more every year,
while you quietly bleed money on gas, repairs, and insurance.

Let's Do the Math

Let's say you buy a $400,000 home with a 30-year mortgage at 7%. By the end of the loan, you'll have paid over $560,000 in interest. That $400K home? It really cost you closer to $970,000. Now let's say you sell it after 30 years for $600,000. That might feel like a win—until you remember inflation. At just 3% per year, that home would need to sell for nearly $970,000 just to match the original value in today's dollars.

So if you sell for $600,000? You didn't build wealth. You lost money.

Let's be generous and say you do sell for $970,000. That's technically a $70,000 "gain" over 30 years. Sounds decent—until you do the math. That's $2,333 per year. About $194 a month. For three decades of ownership, upkeep, taxes, and interest.

That's not passive wealth. That's a low-paying side hustle with roof leaks.

We haven't even touched the hidden costs:

- Property taxes
- HOA fees
- Insurance premiums
- Replacing your roof, plumbing, or AC
- Water damage, mold remediation, pest control
- The $3,000 couch that doesn't fit anywhere else when you move

We've been taught to treat a mortgage like a forced savings plan. But what you're really doing is locking yourself into a high-cost asset with no guaranteed return. That might make sense if you love the home, plan to stay for decades, and can handle the surprises. But if you're banking on it as your primary investment? That's a fragile bet.

That's why I view homes less like investments and more like durable goods. They give you shelter. They offer utility. They create emotional value. But they don't automatically build financial wealth.

You wouldn't finance a car expecting it to grow in value. So why do we pretend homes are different?

They shelter you. They cost money to maintain. Sometimes, they depreciate. Same as a car.

That's still before repairs. Before the busted water heater or the rotting fence. The creeping mold. The cracked foundation. You don't get to ignore those just because the Zillow estimate is higher. That $70K "profit"? It disappears the second real life walks through the door.

The Cost of Chasing Status

One of the biggest drivers of inflated housing costs isn't need—it's ego.

People stretch for nicer places in better neighborhoods not because it makes their lives meaningfully better... but because it looks better. In cities especially, your apartment becomes part of your brand. Where you live is a signal—of success, of taste, of "making it." And that signal comes at a steep cost.

A little status spending can be fine, but housing is a dangerous place to flex. A slightly trendier zip code or upgraded kitchen might mean less travel, fewer savings, or no room for emergencies. You sacrifice long-term financial stability to look stable in the short term.

And here's the real trap: once you lock in a lease or mortgage at that level, it's hard to go backwards—even if it's the smartest thing for your finances. Downsizing feels like failure. Getting a roommate feels like regression. So instead of making the move

that would actually give them freedom, people stay stuck—in a place that's slowly bleeding them dry.
The truth? Your zip code doesn't determine your worth.
Your peace does.

My Housing Rule: The $1,000 Cap

For most of my adult life, I had a hard rule: never pay more than $1,000 a month in rent.

It didn't matter that I lived in big cities. It didn't matter what my friends were paying. That rule was the anchor that kept my finances from drifting. I made one exception—and it was to help someone else. But otherwise, I stuck to it.
That one decision shaped everything.

It capped my housing cost at about $33/day. That meant more flexibility for groceries, travel, debt payoff, saving, fun, and unexpected expenses. It meant I could live fully without living recklessly.

And yes, it meant I had roommates. Almost always. Here's what no one tells you: having a roommate doesn't just cut your rent—it changes your entire financial trajectory. It also ties you into community. Sharing costs means sharing life—meals, stories, even support when things get rough. We often think of roommates as a downgrade, but in reality, they're one of the clearest examples of how community makes individual finances stronger. It gives you margin. Stability. In a lot of cases, companionship that makes life more fun.
Let's say you live alone in a $1,600 apartment. That's about $53/day. But split a $2,000 two-bedroom with someone else? You're paying $1,000, or $33/day. That's $20/day back in your pocket. That's $600/month you can reallocate to freedom.

I know some people swear by the "30% of income" rule. My version was simpler: don't pay over $1,000/month in rent unless you're making six figures. Even then, think twice.

It sounds aggressive. It was. But it worked. It protected me from lifestyle creep. It kept me in control. It reminded me that financial success isn't about appearances—it's about options.

Also… let's be real: roommates come with side benefits. Like reducing the risk of choking on popcorn with no one around to save you.

Don't Over-Correct

It's tempting to hear advice like mine and swing too far the other way—moving an hour outside the city, buying a cheap fixer-upper in a neighborhood you don't feel safe in, or locking into a long lease in a place you don't even like… all in the name of "being smart."

But savings aren't savings if they cost you your sanity.

If your rent is cheap but your commute steals three hours a day, or you're too far from your friends, or your apartment leaves you anxious or isolated? That's not a good deal. That's just a different kind of expensive.

Your housing decision should reduce your stress—not just your spending.

Because the goal isn't to beat the system by punishing yourself. The goal is to create a life you can afford and enjoy. That might still mean sacrifice—but it shouldn't feel like exile.

That's not frugal. That's expensive in a different currency—your time, your energy, your mental health.

If You're Going to Buy…

Full transparency: I've never owned a home. But if I did? I'd apply the same mindset I've used with renting—low cost, high flexibility, and zero delusion about what a house can or can't do for me financially.

If you're going to buy, buy with clarity—not fantasy. That means:

- Pay it down as fast as possible. The faster you knock out interest, the faster the home becomes a tool instead of a trap.
- House hack early. A roommate, a partner, a friend— someone to split costs with, even temporarily. That's not just smart. That's protection.
- Treat it like a tool, not a lottery ticket. Your home isn't your big break. It's your base. Use it wisely, but don't bet your future on its value rising forever.

If you split the mortgage early, you lower your risk and boost your options. You're not crushed when the water heater breaks. You're not panicking when property taxes jump. You've got a buffer—because you built one.

Owning a home can be a great decision. But only if you walk in with eyes wide open.

Don't fall for the idea that it's automatically better. It's not. It's just different.

In some cases, renting may actually give you more control over your financial future than owning ever could.

Where Renters Insurance Fits

If you're renting, here's one cost you can't really avoid: renters insurance. Most landlords mandate it, and even if they don't, you should carry it anyway. It's cheap—often \$10–20 a month—and it protects you against disasters you can't predict: fire, theft, water damage. For the price of a couple of streaming subscriptions, you buy yourself peace of mind that your stuff can be replaced if life takes a swing at you. Think of it less as an optional add-on and more as part of your baseline housing cost.

Housing Audit: A Quick Challenge

Take five minutes and answer these questions—no spreadsheets, no calculators, just brutal honesty:

- What percentage of your take-home pay goes to housing right now?
- Could you reduce that by 20% if you had to?
- Are you living alone because you need the peace—or because it feels like "success"?
- If you had to move tomorrow, would you choose the same setup again?

This isn't about shame. It's about sight.

Because until you look housing square in the face—not the fantasy, not the real estate photos, but the actual cost—you can't steer your budget. If you can't steer your budget, you're not in control.

Without control, freedom is just a feeling—not a plan.

Chapter 5: Overspending is Under-Thinking

L et's face it—if you're reading this book, you're probably not beating yourself up over every dollar you've spent. You're beating yourself up over why you spent it.

That's okay. Let's start by forgiving that. Overspending isn't always about indulgence. Most of the time, it's about uncertainty—a lack of context, a lack of visibility, a lack of real math.

You're not broke because of a $5 coffee. Vince Young didn't go bankrupt after earning over $25 million in NFL contracts because of weekly Cheesecake Factory binges. Overspending—whether it's lattes or lobster—isn't the core issue. The real problem is spending without understanding.

Until now, no one gave you a real framework. No one showed you how your passive spend (rent, insurance, subscriptions) quietly caps your active spend—the money you use to live. So you move through life guessing, hoping, trying not to look too closely.

But when you start doing the math? The game changes. You begin to see that every dollar has a purpose—or a consequence.

Maybe your passive spending is so high you've only got $10/day left for everything else: food, gas, social life. That's survival mode. Every dollar has to be surgical. On the flip side, maybe you've got $50+/day in breathing room. That's freedom to move—but it still demands intention.

That $5 coffee? It's not the villain. But if you're already stretched thin, that $1,825/year deserves a second look.

Same goes for Vince Young. Let's say he cleared $10 million after taxes. If he spent $5,000/week at Cheesecake Factory, he could've kept that up for 38 years. The issue wasn't the appetizers—it was everything else. Lack of context. Lack of limits.

Overspending isn't failure. It's fog.

Let's clear it.

The Return-on-Spend Mindset

One way I've stayed financially grounded is by running mental math on purchases—even the small ones.

When I was 23, I was earning about $28,500 a year. After taxes, that worked out to around $10/hour. That number became my baseline for value. A $15 movie? That's 90 minutes of entertainment for 90 minutes of work—fair trade. But a 90-minute movie with a $15 ticket and another $15 in popcorn and drinks? Now we're talking three hours of work for an hour and a half of passive fun. That math didn't always line up.

That doesn't mean you can't spend on joy—it just means you should know what it's costing you.

Even now, I run those calculations. I have AMC A-List because I love movies, and the monthly fee gives me access to multiple showings each week. It's a high-ROI purchase for me because I actually use it—and because it aligns with how I relax and recharge.

But this mindset isn't just for $15 purchases. It's even more important for the medium-tier ones—the ones that cost a few hundred dollars, feel productive or exciting, and end up collecting dust.

Take the pandemic-era stand mixer craze. Let's say you bought a $300 mixer to make dough. If mixing manually takes five minutes, and the machine saves you that time, you'd need to use it 360 times just to save 30 hours—the break-even point if your time is worth $10/hour.

Be honest. Are you really baking 360 times?

This is what I call Spend ROI. It's not about guilt—it's about alignment. You're not asking whether you deserve something. You're asking whether it pays off in time, value, or repeated use. Does it earn its place in your life?

Value isn't just the price tag. It's how often you use it, how much it improves your daily life, and whether it reflects your priorities—not your impulses.

The "Before You Buy" Checklist

Here's a quick gut check before you swipe, click, or tap "Buy Now." Run through a few of these first:

- Will I use this at least 10 times? If not, can I rent or borrow it instead?
- What's the hourly joy or utility? Would I trade an hour of my time to own it?
- Is this solving a real problem—or just buying a feeling? Am I curing boredom with boxes on my doorstep?
- Is the upgrade really worth it? Is a $1,200 phone actually twice as good as the $600 one?

These aren't hard rules—but they are honest ones. If your answers feel shaky, defensive, or avoidant?

You probably don't need it.

A Medium-Tier Spending Mistake (and Lesson)

Here's one I'll own.

Like many during the pandemic, I bought a stand mixer. I envisioned baking fresh bread, crafting pizza dough, maybe even making homemade pasta. It looked great on the counter and felt like a smart investment in domesticity. But in reality, it just sat there.

We used it a handful of times. Mostly, it was modern kitchen art —taking up space and whispering promises it never fulfilled.

Assuming it cost $300 and saved five minutes per use, with only ten uses, that's 50 minutes saved—less than an hour. Valuing my time at $10/hour, that's a $290 loss.

The mixer wasn't faulty; I bought into the idea of being someone who bakes. I liked the image it projected, the routine I imagined around it. But I didn't need it, nor did I use it enough to justify the expense.

That's under-thinking: purchasing for the lifestyle you hope to create instead of the one you're actually living.

But here's the flip side.

I also bought an Apple Watch—Series 4—back in 2018. I'm still using that same watch today, with just one battery replacement. As of now, Apple has released the Series 10, meaning I've skipped six upgrade cycles.

This watch tracks my movement, reminds me to stand, and holds me accountable to my habits. Since I started using it, I've lost 35 pounds from my peak pandemic weight.

That purchase didn't transform my life overnight. But it supported the changes I was committed to making. And that's the difference.

Small Spend, Big Impact

Now let's bring it back to the little things.

We've all heard the "cut the lattes" argument. It's overplayed, often patronizing, and mostly misses the point. A $5 coffee isn't why you can't afford a home. But it might be why you can't afford a spontaneous trip. Or why your emergency fund never grows. Or why your credit card balance doesn't budge.

Let's take food delivery as another example. If you regularly order lunch for $20 a pop, five times a week, that's $100 a week —$5,200 a year. That's a used car. A serious dent in your student loans. An IRA contribution. A flight home to see your family— twice.

Now back to coffee.

Daily lattes add up too. But you don't have to cut them cold turkey. You just need a smarter system. I'll give you mine: I brew Kauai Coffee at home using 6 rounded tablespoons per pot from an $8 bag. I make it in a Hamilton Beach coffee maker I bought back in 2015 for $81.83, and pour it into a 40-ounce Thermos I picked up for $29.99. That one pot lasts me two days. My cost per pot? About 86 cents. That's 43 cents a day.

Over a year, that adds up to about $158. Compare that to $5/ day at Starbucks, which comes out to $1,825/year—and I'm saving about $1,667 annually. Just on coffee.

That doesn't mean I never buy Starbucks. I still grab a cup now and then—but it's the exception, not the routine. Because I've already built a system that works the other 360 days a year.

It's not about deprivation. It's about design.

This isn't about guilt. It's about options.

If you know the tradeoff and choose it anyway? Fine. That's intentional spending.

But if you're falling behind and haven't run the math? Then yeah—you're overspending by under-thinking. You're trading progress for convenience, without even realizing it.

Those small daily habits? They don't just nibble at your budget. Over time, they chew right through your future.

The Trap of "It's Just…"

"It's just $15."
"It's just a $30 subscription."
"It's just one dinner out."

Those little phrases? They're the footnotes of financial denial. "It's just" is how we excuse patterns. It's how we dodge reflection. It's how we give ourselves permission to spend without thinking.
But ten "justs" in a week? That's a few hundred dollars. They add up faster than you want to believe.

Let's say you subscribe to three streaming services, order delivery twice a week, buy one impulse item from Amazon every weekend, and grab a coffee every weekday. None of it feels huge. But altogether? That's easily $400 a month. Over $4,800 a year.

That's not "just" anything. That's not a footnote—it's a headline. And if you're not careful, it becomes the main story of your financial life.

You don't have to cut everything. But you do have to stop pretending that "just" means harmless.

Because when you repeat a small expense often enough, it stops being small. It becomes automatic. And once your spending is automatic, your awareness disappears.

That's when trouble starts.

The Lottery Isn't a Plan—It's a Tax on Hope

People say the lottery is harmless fun—a small chance at a big win. But in reality, it's a stealth tax on the people who can least afford it.

Americans spend over $113 billion a year on lottery tickets—around $437 per adult. Low-income households spend the most, often nearly four times as much as wealthier families.

Here's the kicker: you're more likely to be struck by lightning than win a big jackpot. And scratch-offs? Nearly half the money spent goes right back into someone else's pocket. It's not entertainment—it's engineered to take.
Meanwhile, that $437 could have funded unexpected bills, padded your emergency fund, or chipped away at debt. But the system sells you hope so you don't build something real.

I'm not saying never buy a ticket. I'm saying don't fool yourself into thinking it's a plan. Because gambling is just another system built to keep you spending… until you have nothing left.

Think in Tradeoffs, Not Shame

This chapter isn't about shame. It's about understanding that every dollar is a tradeoff.

A $120 dinner might be worth it—if you're celebrating something rare, if it brings joy, if it creates a memory.
But a $120 Costco run where half the stuff ends up forgotten in the back of the pantry? Probably not.

This is where intentionality beats budgeting apps. You don't need to log every transaction if you pause long enough to ask yourself:

- Do I value this more than the thing I say I want long-term?
- Would Future Me thank me… or shake their head?

Overspending isn't always about bad judgment. Sometimes it's just speed. Distraction. Habit.

The solution isn't guilt. It's pause.

A breath before the tap.
A question before the swipe.
A moment of thought before the momentum takes over.
That one pause? It's the difference between spending reactively and spending on purpose.

Rewire the Swipe

Here's your assignment.

This week, pick one purchase you're about to make. It doesn't matter if it's a $5 drink or a $500 gadget. Before you buy it, pause. Ask yourself:

- Will this actually improve my life?
- Can I afford it and still meet my goals?
- Is this solving a problem—or chasing a feeling?

Then—whatever your answer—own it.

If you still want the thing? Go for it. But go in with your eyes open. Not because some finance guru told you to skip it… but because you understand your math.

Overspending isn't always irresponsible.
Sometimes, it's just unconscious.

Let's change that.

Chapter 6: The Big Ticket Trap

Some spending choices fade into the background. Others drive your entire financial future.

That's what big-ticket purchases do. They aren't "just" decisions about cars, college, or where you live. They're structural. They turn into anchors—or accelerators. If you don't choose them with clarity, they'll quietly decide the rest of your life for you.

You won't feel it the day you sign the loan.
You'll feel it when you can't change jobs because the payment's too high.
You'll feel it when the interest starts stacking faster than your savings.
You'll feel it when your rent goes up, but you can't afford to move.

These choices—cars, degrees, homes—don't live in your latte budget. They don't show up in daily expenses. But they dominate your passive spending for years. Maybe decades.

They feel responsible. Adult. Even aspirational.
But if you get one wrong... your future doesn't bend. It buckles.

A $5 coffee won't change your life.
A $50,000 decision will.

The Car You Think You Deserve

Let's talk about status on wheels.

A friend of mine once considered buying a $46,000 BMW X1. She worked from home three days a week, drove her kids to school on a short loop, and already had a reliable car with less than 50,000 miles on it. Her income was solid—about $115K/year, or roughly $41/hour after taxes—and her actual time behind the wheel each week? Less than two hours.

It wasn't about need. It was about perception. Comfort. Maybe even identity.

But when we ran the math, the story changed.

That car would need to last her more than 11 years to be "worth it" based on usage. Meanwhile, keeping her current car would free up $4,000 per year—money that could fund family vacations before her kids went off to college. Once she saw it through that lens, the BMW lost its shine.

This is the trap. Overspending on cars doesn't look like a neon-red mistake. It looks reasonable. Quiet. It's not about Ferraris and flexing. It's about buying "nicer" because your old car feels "used," even when it runs perfectly fine.

Big-ticket spending rarely screams, "I'm a bad choice." It whispers, "You've earned this."
That's what makes it dangerous.

Leasing: The Trap That Never Ends

Leasing sounds smart—lower payments, newer cars, fewer headaches. But behind the sleek pitch is a simple reality: you're paying for the privilege of never owning anything.

Leasing guarantees one thing—you will always have a car payment.

That means your monthly budget is locked into a cost that never disappears. Sure, the car is new. Sure, maintenance is covered—for now. But every few years, you start over. You don't escape the treadmill… you sign back up.

There's no payoff moment. No debt-free chapter. Just a permanent rental agreement with nicer seats.

Let's not forget the long game:

Leasing for 10 years could easily cost you $40,000–$60,000... with zero equity to show for it.

That money doesn't build anything. It just disappears. Worse, it normalizes the idea that transportation should always cost you hundreds a month, forever.

That's not adulthood. That's entrapment.

I'd rather buy a reliable used car, drive it into the ground, and give my monthly budget the freedom to move on.

If You're Going to Buy a Car...

- Choose reliability over luxury or tech.
- Run the numbers: are you spending $30K for something you'll use three hours a week?
- Avoid 72-, 84-, or 96-month loans. By the time you're done paying, the car's already old—and you've likely shelled out thousands extra in interest over 6+ years.
- Don't treat a paid-off car as an excuse to upgrade. Let that "no payment" phase be the goal.
- Redirect that old car payment toward something better— savings, travel, breathing room.

Cars are tools. They're not milestones, they're not trophies, and they're definitely not investments.

Use them. Don't get used by them.

Education: Your Most Underrated Investment (or Mistake)

Education might be the most expensive gamble you ever make. And like all big-ticket decisions, its danger lies in how reasonable it seems.

Degrees are framed as investments. And sometimes, they are. But not automatically.

I'm not anti-college. I'm anti-casual-debt.

The return on education depends on two things:

- How much it costs
- What it earns you

If the numbers don't add up, neither will your budget.

A $120,000 degree that leads to a $48,000 job isn't a pathway to freedom—it's a delayed financial penalty. And if that degree doesn't lead to a job at all? You've just signed up for one of the worst deals in modern life: high-cost, low-yield debt that never goes away.

As of late 2024, median in-state tuition at public colleges is under $10K/year. That means a community college transfer path—two years at $2K, two years at $10K—can get you the same diploma for under $25,000.

Don't confuse educational access with financial wisdom.

You don't need to spend $100,000 to prove you're serious.

That's not ambition. That's a setup.

Adult Education Is a Secret Weapon

Community colleges aren't just for teenagers. They're built for working adults, career switchers, side hustlers, and anyone trying to level up without going broke.

They offer:

- Certifications
- Trade programs
- Associate degrees
- Night classes
- Online flexibility

They do it all at a fraction of the price of traditional universities
—or shady for-profit schools.

If you're even considering a new path, start here. It's low-cost,
low-risk, and publicly funded.
You're already paying for it through taxes.
Use it.

For-Profit Colleges: A Red Flag

If the name sounds like a brand… walk away.
If the ad runs between car insurance and payday loans… run
faster.

For-profit colleges are expert marketers—but terrible educators.
They target low-income students, single parents, and veterans
with promises of flexibility and fast-track careers.

What they actually deliver:

- Bloated tuition
- Worthless degrees
- High dropout rates
- Lifelong debt

These places aren't built to teach you.
They're built to bill you.

You deserve better.

Avoid them.

Housing: The Longest Commitment

Rent feels like a monthly decision—but it's really a multi-year financial shape-shifter.

$2,000/month might sound manageable today… but over five years? That's $120,000. It often rises faster than your income. Housing becomes the quiet siphon that drains opportunity—not because you overspent once, but because it never stops.

Owning sounds like the smarter path. But a mortgage is a marathon of hidden costs.

A $400,000 home at 7% interest? That's over $500,000 in interest alone—bringing your true cost close to $900,000 over 30 years.

You're not just buying a house. You're committing to a lifetime of property taxes, repairs, maintenance, and surprises that rarely come cheap.

That's before you fix the roof, replace the water heater, or cover the inevitable HOA fee spike.

Rent-Free Isn't Risk-Free

Living at home? Crashing with family or a partner rent-free?

That's not a loophole—it's a window.

Don't waste it.

Use that time to:

- Pay off high-interest debt
- Build a savings cushion
- Invest in a credential or skill that changes your earning power

If someone's keeping the lights on for you, show gratitude with action—help out financially, cover groceries, pitch in on bills.

Support might feel free. But dignity asks you to contribute.

There's no such thing as truly free housing.

The Housing Flex Tradeoff

I used to live by a rule: never pay more than $1,000/month in rent until I owned.

Why? Because that number gave me room to breathe. To save. To choose.

Break it down: $1,000/month is about $33 a day—or $1.40 an hour—to have a roof over your head. When you look at it hourly, it forces real questions:

- Would you live with a roommate to save $400/month?
- Would you downsize to avoid debt or afford a trip?
- Are you living alone because it brings peace—or because it looks impressive?

Housing flex is expensive. Sometimes it's worth it. But you should know why you're paying what you're paying.

Don't let lifestyle inflation hide behind granite countertops.

Tradeoffs don't disappear when you earn more.
They just get bigger.

The Big Ticket Test

Before any major purchase, ask yourself:

- Will this last longer than the loan I'm taking on?
- What if my usable income dropped by 50%—could I still afford it?
- Am I buying this because it helps me... or because it impresses someone?
- Will I still be glad I did this five years from now?

That 50% drop might not come from job loss—it might come from a medical bill, an emergency, or just life showing up uninvited. Either way, the pressure hits the same place: your budget.

If those questions make you hesitate... pause harder.
Clarity is more valuable than convenience.

Final Thoughts: One Misstep, One Decade

One overpriced degree.
One car lease that turned into two.
One mortgage you weren't quite ready for.

That's all it takes to trap a decade.

Not because you made a wild mistake—but because you never stopped to ask the right questions before locking in a cost you couldn't easily escape.

That's how the Big Ticket Trap gets you.
It doesn't feel like overspending—it feels like growing up.
It feels like doing the "smart" thing... until you're stuck rearranging your whole life around a payment.

So take the pause. Run the numbers.
Ask harder questions before you sign anything long-term.

Because building real freedom isn't about skipping coffee or budgeting every snack.

It's about being ruthlessly clear on the big ticket ones.

Chapter 7: The True Cost of a Loan

I t's easy to grasp active spending. Swipe your card, watch your balance drop. It's immediate. It's visible. You feel it.

Loans are sneakier. They delay the pain. They stretch it out.

That's the danger.

A loan isn't just a purchase—it's a time capsule of regret waiting to open. It turns one financial decision into years of fixed obligation. You stop paying for what you bought—and start paying for the permission to have bought it early.

The result? You give away your future flexibility in exchange for today's convenience.

That might be worth it—sometimes.
But most people don't stop to ask what it really costs them down the line.

Let's break it down by the types of loans you probably interact with most often—and why they require sharper thinking than most people give them.

Buy Now, Pay Later: Layaway's Flashy Cousin

Buy Now, Pay Later—BNPL—is everywhere now. Clothing, electronics, even groceries. Instead of paying upfront, you're offered four "easy" payments. No interest. No credit check. No friction.

It feels modern. Responsible, even. A smarter way to budget.

But it's not budgeting. It's debt—just repackaged to feel like convenience.

The payment plan is simple:

- 25% now
- 25% two weeks later
- Then two more payments, each spaced out
- If you miss one? There are often fees or auto-debits that hit your account without warning

Used sparingly, BNPL can help in a pinch. But most people don't use it sparingly.

They use it to stack purchases they couldn't otherwise afford. Since it doesn't show up on your credit report, there's no built-in ceiling—no warning light when you've gone too far. You can easily have five or six BNPL plans active at once, each quietly eating away at your cash flow.

It's not that one payment will hurt you.
It's that the pile-up happens fast—and silently.

This isn't layaway. It's the illusion of affordability with none of the guardrails.

Used thoughtfully, it can give you breathing room.
Used casually, it takes it away.

If you're not careful, you're not stretching your budget.
You're just stretching the timeline for regret.

Real Talk: A Composite BNPL Cautionary Tale

Let's walk through what this looks like in real life.

Someone buys a $200 winter jacket. A week later, they add a $150 pair of headphones. Then a $300 airline ticket. Then a $100 bundle of skincare products. None of it feels outrageous. In fact, it feels smart—they're spacing it out.

The total? $750.

They only put down 25% up front—$187.50. Manageable, right? But over the next six weeks, they owe the other $562.50… on top of rent, groceries, and bills. If they did this across two or three BNPL platforms, the payments won't even hit at the same time. There's no single "due date" to manage—it's a stream of withdrawals across multiple apps.

They didn't sit down and plan to take on $750 in debt. They just clicked "Pay Later" a few times.

That's what makes BNPL so dangerous. It's not labeled as debt. It doesn't trigger the same emotional red flags. But financially? It behaves the same way.

This is how debt sneaks in—without ever saying its name.

Credit Cards: One-Month Loans with a Trapdoor

Credit cards are everywhere. They're handed out at campus events, offered at checkout counters, and framed as a mark of adulthood. On the surface, they seem like a smart financial tool —buy now, pay later, build credit, earn points.

But the truth is this: a credit card is just a one-month loan. If you pay it off in full, it works. If you don't, it turns on you. Interest rates often hover between 18–25%. That means carrying a $1,000 balance could cost you over $200 a year—just for the privilege of borrowing your own future money. A $50 dinner becomes a $63 charge if you let it ride.

The trap isn't just the math. It's psychological:

- The money doesn't feel real—it's not cash in your hand
- The points and perks feel like rewards
- The minimum payment feels like progress, even when it's not

Minimum payments are designed to keep you in debt. They make it look like you're chipping away at your balance, when in reality, you're mostly covering interest. It's a slow bleed that becomes your new normal.

That doesn't mean credit cards are evil. Used wisely, they can build credit history, offer protection against fraud, and provide useful benefits. But they only help you if you stay in control.

A credit card isn't free money—it's a pre-approved loan with marketing flair.

Use it like a debit card with perks. Pay in full. Track what you spend. Know that the convenience isn't worth it if it comes at the cost of your freedom.

The Balance-Carrying Lie

There's a myth that just won't die:

"You have to carry a balance to build credit."

Nope. False. Completely made up.
In reality, carrying a balance means you're paying interest for no reason. You're giving your bank extra money each month… and getting nothing in return.

You do not need to carry debt to build credit.
You just need to:

- Use your card regularly
- Keep your usage under 30% of your limit
- Pay the full statement balance by the due date

That last part matters more than people think.

Let's say you charged $500 total this month. But your statement balance—the official amount due—is $400. That's the number to focus on. If you pay that $400 in full and on time, you avoid interest and your credit score improves.

You don't need to pay the extra $100 that posted after the statement closed. That amount isn't due yet—and paying it early doesn't boost your score. It just moves money faster than necessary.

The trap is thinking "more is better." But credit doesn't reward you for overpaying—it rewards you for paying on time and in full.

Carrying a balance won't help your credit.
It just makes your bank richer.

The Minimum Payment Scam

Let's say you have a $2,000 balance on a credit card with a 19.99% APR.

If you only make the minimum payment each month—say, $40 to $50—it could take over 18 years to pay it off. By the time you're done, you'll have paid more than $4,000 total… double what you originally spent.

That's not a glitch. That's the business model.

Credit card companies want you to pay the minimum. They design your statement to make that number look like a suggestion. A baseline. A path forward.

But it's not. It's a trap door.

Minimum payments are the slowest, most expensive way to eliminate debt. And they're built to look helpful.

It's not guidance—it's bait.

Medium-Term Loans: Affordable Payments, Expensive Mistakes

These are the quiet ones. Car loans. Furniture financing. Medical procedures. Even vacations.

They don't feel like dangerous debt because the monthly payment looks reasonable. You might borrow $5,000 and agree to pay $106 a month for five years. That feels doable—safe, even.

But here's the trick: you're not just buying the item. You're buying time... and you're paying for it.
A $5,000 loan at 10% interest over five years means you'll pay $6,374 in total. That's $1,374 in interest—just for spreading it out. Early on, most of your payments go toward interest, not principal.

Now imagine you could afford $150/month instead of $106:

- You'd finish the loan nearly two years early
- You'd save close to $500 in interest
- You'd reclaim that monthly cash flow much sooner

This isn't just about saving money. It's about regaining flexibility.

Most loans are front-loaded with interest. The earlier you pay extra, the more damage you do—in a good way.

You're shrinking the timeline and the total cost.

Refinance Isn't a Dirty Word

Refinancing gets a bad rap—like it's something you only do if you've made a mistake. But smart borrowers revisit their debt when conditions change.

I helped someone refinance their student loans. They were paying over 7% interest with years left to go. By switching to a lower rate and choosing a shorter term, they saved more than $1,000 in interest and shaved years off the repayment timeline.

That's not failure. That's strategy.

If rates drop or your credit improves, it's worth running the numbers again. You might qualify for a better deal—one that frees up cash or shortens your payoff window.

Loans shouldn't be "set and forget."
They should evolve as your life and finances do.

The Illusion of Affordability

Most people don't ask, "Can I afford the total cost of this loan?" They ask, "Can I swing the monthly payment?"

That's how the trap is set.

A $400/month car payment might sound completely reasonable. But over five years, that's $24,000—before interest, insurance, gas, and repairs. Add it all up, and what looked like a manageable line item becomes a major drag on your budget.

This is how someone making $80,000 a year can still feel broke. Every raise gets swallowed by past decisions. Every new opportunity is weighed against existing obligations. The monthly bills win—again.

They haven't overspent once.
They've overspent slowly.

They've mistaken cash flow for capacity.

Before You Borrow... Ask Yourself

Whether it's a Buy Now, Pay Later plan, a credit card swipe, or a five-year personal loan—pause for a moment and run through these questions:

- Would I still want this if I had to pay the full amount today?
- Can I comfortably pay more than the minimum each month?
- Is this something I need... or something I want right now?
- What's the total amount I'll repay, including interest?

These aren't trick questions. They're clarity questions.

If the answers make you pause, that's your answer.

You already know.

Final Note: Your Money Has a Memory

Every loan you take on leaves a fingerprint on your future.

It's not just about the payments. It's about the pressure. A loan changes your options. It limits your ability to pivot, take risks, or walk away from a bad situation. It turns future income into past decisions.

That doesn't mean all loans are bad. Some create real value—a car that opens job opportunities, a degree that boosts earning power, a renovation that improves quality of life. But those decisions need to be made with full awareness.

Because when a loan is taken casually, the consequences aren't. The bill always comes—just not right away.

So before you borrow, pause.

Run the numbers.
Ask the questions.

Your future self is watching.

Chapter 8: The Education Fallacy

Are you a high school graduate? Congrats. As of 2024, you've joined the 94% of Americans who hold that diploma, according to the Institute of Education Sciences. A generation ago, that was the starting line for adulthood. Today? It's barely the warm-up.

Because now comes the pressure to level up—fast.

The expectation is clear: go to college, take out loans, and trust the payoff will come. More school equals more success. That's the story we've all been told—by parents, guidance counselors, pop culture, and government policy.

But here's the truth: while education can be one of the best investments you ever make… it can also be a quietly devastating financial trap.

And that trap isn't just personal—it's generational. Remember my hypothesis—*Economic Distance*? This is one of the clearest examples. Your grandparents don't always realize it, but the few hundred dollars they paid for college in the 1960s would now equal tens of thousands. According to the National Center for Education Statistics, the average annual cost of tuition, fees, room, and board at a public university rose from about $930 in 1963 to over $25,000 today—a jump of roughly 2,600%. Private universities climbed from around $2,000 to more than $55,000—up over 2,700%. Meanwhile, median household income only grew by about 900%.

What changed wasn't just tuition—it was who paid for it. From the late 1970s through the 1980s, a wave of federal and state tax cuts shifted the cost of higher education away from government budgets and onto individual families. Public colleges that were once 70%–80% publicly funded became less than 25% publicly funded. Grants shrank. Loans filled the gap. The result? A generational hand-off of cost that widened the very gap I have been describing.

You can trace a lot of that shift back to California. When Ronald Reagan became governor in 1967, he cut funding for public universities, pushed for the first meaningful tuition in the University of California system, and said taxpayers shouldn't be asked to "subsidize intellectual curiosity." That moment was a turning point. What began as a state experiment became a national philosophy—education reframed as a private investment rather than a public good. When Reagan carried that mindset to Washington a decade later, federal grants shrank, student loans ballooned, and the generational divide in opportunity deepened.

Economists love to measure tuition year over year, as if a 4% increase tells the story. It doesn't. The real story stretches across sixty years—three generations of shrinking public investment, deregulation, and wage stagnation that turned what was once a public good into a private gamble. **That's the true measure of** *Economic Distance*—**and why education now builds debt faster than it builds opportunity.**

This book isn't about making more money. It's about managing what you have and avoiding the worst outcomes. Education is one of those major costs—like housing or a car—that can either move you forward or leave you stuck for decades.

Not All Degrees Are Created Equal

There's a stat that gets tossed around a lot: over a lifetime, college graduates earn about $1 million more than those with just a high school diploma.

It sounds convincing. But it hides the truth.

That number is an average—and averages are dangerous when they blur the extremes. The actual return on a degree depends on what you study, whether you finish, and how much you borrow to get there.

Here's the part most people don't hear: according to the U.S. Department of Education, roughly four in ten students who start a four-year degree don't graduate within six years. That's not a minor detail. That's almost half. And if you take out loans but don't get the diploma? You're left with the debt—but none of the earnings boost.

It's like buying a car and then totaling it—you're still on the hook for the payments, but you don't get to drive anywhere.

So before you enroll—especially at a private or out-of-state school—ask yourself a few critical questions:

- Do I know what kind of career I actually want?
- Have I looked up the average starting salary in that field?
- Have I compared the total cost of attendance across multiple schools?

If the answer to any of those is "no," then you're not ready to sign for tens of thousands in debt. You might still want to explore—and that's okay—but you need to do it affordably.

Start at Community College: Low Cost, High Flexibility

Community colleges are one of the most underrated tools in the entire education system. They give you time to figure out your path, build transferable credits, and gain valuable skills—all without wrecking your finances.

Here's what makes them powerful:

- You can complete general education requirements at a fraction of the cost
- You can live at home or work part-time while attending
- You get access to professors, advisors, and career programs just like at a four-year school

If you transfer later? The degree says the name of the university you finish at—not the place you started.

That same bachelor's degree from a $60,000/year private school? You can earn it for less than $25,000 total—just for thousands less.

But there's a catch…

The Credit Transfer Trap

A lot of students start at community college with the intention to transfer. It's a smart move—until they discover that not all their credits come with them.

This isn't just bad luck. It's a structural problem.

Many four-year institutions don't want your transfer credits. Not because they aren't valid, but because letting them in means less tuition for the university. The result? Students who follow the rules still end up having to retake courses, delay graduation, and pay more—sometimes thousands more.

It's a system designed to create friction.
It punishes the people trying to do things the smart way.

Even when they did everything right.

We need policy reform here.

If you're a voter, a parent, or someone who cares about economic mobility, this is one of the clearest fights we should be having: push your state to adopt universal credit transfer laws.

That one change would radically improve access to affordable higher education. It would eliminate duplication, reduce time to graduation, and save families tens of thousands of dollars.

It wouldn't fix everything. But it would fix a lot.

If every state adopted a clear, transferable general education core—no exceptions, no fine print—community college would become the smartest financial on-ramp to a degree for millions.

Questions to Ask Before Choosing a School

Before you commit to any college or university, ask:

- What's the total cost—including housing, fees, and living expenses?
- What percentage of students graduate within 6 years? (According to the National Center for Education Statistics, only 41% of full-time students earn a bachelor's degree in four years—so if a school brags about its "four-year program," look deeper.)
- What's the average starting salary for my intended major?
- Is the school regionally accredited?
- Can I live at home or do I need to move?
- Are there public alternatives with the same or similar programs?

You don't need to know every answer—but you should like the ones you find. If you don't, it's not a reason to panic—it's a reason to pause.

Step back and reconsider.
Education is too expensive to leave to chance.

Community Colleges > For-Profit Trade Schools

If you're considering a trade or skill-based path—electrician, mechanic, dental assistant, software developer—you don't need to take on $20,000 in debt at a shiny private program with slick marketing.

Start with your local community college.

They often offer the exact same certifications and hands-on training—sometimes with better employer partnerships and lower class sizes. And because they're publicly funded, they're built to serve you, not to profit from you.

Community colleges often include:

- Lower tuition
- Training programs aligned with local job demand
- Built-in business courses if you want to freelance or start your own shop
- Smaller class sizes and more instructor access
- Access to federal aid and public resources

It's not just the smart choice. It's the sustainable one.

You're already funding them with your taxes. Use them.

Avoid For-Profit Universities at All Costs

Let's be blunt: for-profit universities are built to sell debt, not deliver education.

They target low-income students, single parents, veterans—anyone looking for a second chance or a fast track. Their promises are everywhere: flexible scheduling, guaranteed job placement, personalized attention. But what they deliver is often a different story:

- High tuition
- Low graduation rates
- Unrecognized or unaccredited degrees
- Poor job placement
- Massive loan burdens

Worse, many students leave without a degree—but still owe tens of thousands of dollars. Those credits? Often non-transferable. The school got paid. You got stuck.
These institutions exist because we allowed higher education to become a private market. Their business model depends on federal aid—not outcomes.

Unless you're looking at a public college or a well-reviewed nonprofit with transparent graduation and employment stats, walk away. Always check for regional accreditation—not just "licensed" or "certified."

Employers know the difference.
So should you.

Public State Schools = Smart, Scalable, Successful

If you're set on a four-year degree, look at your state's public university system first. These schools are built for scale—and built with your tax dollars. They're often just as rigorous as private institutions, but at a fraction of the cost.

I grew up in New York, where the SUNY system offers dozens of respected programs. California has the CSU and UC systems. These aren't second-tier schools—they're smart, affordable, and often lead to the exact same job opportunities as private colleges that charge triple the tuition.

I didn't take that path.

I pushed my mom—who was a retired teacher—to send me to Syracuse University, a private school that cost $50,000 a year. I had a dream: walk onto the lacrosse team, play at the highest level, and win a national championship.

And I did.

That's something no spreadsheet can capture. It shaped my identity. It taught me how to show up, even when I wasn't the star. It gave me four unforgettable years.

But outside of lacrosse? I didn't have much of a plan. I picked my major because a friend of mine said she was going to do it. Eventually, I found my way into classes I actually cared about—but I burned through a lot of tuition before I got there.

Was it worth it emotionally? Without a doubt.
Was it worth it financially? That's more complicated.

The debt didn't just impact my wallet.
It narrowed my choices.

Grad School: Prestige Won't Pay the Bills

Thinking about graduate school? Pause before you chase the name on the diploma.

Some master's degrees are necessary—teaching, counseling, nursing, certain social work roles. And in those cases, the focus should be on affordability, not prestige. Most employers care more about your license and experience than the logo on your transcripts.

Other programs—MBAs, MFAs, JDs—can absolutely open doors. I went the MBA route myself. It gave me tools, confidence, and access to opportunities I wouldn't have found otherwise.

But even with the right program, there's a tradeoff. Tuition can reach six figures, and not every program delivers a clear return. The letters after your name don't guarantee a pay bump—especially if the degree wasn't aligned with a specific path.

So if you're considering grad school, look beyond the branding.

Ask:

- Will this increase my income in a meaningful, lasting way?
- Will it pay for itself within five years?
- Is there a public or part-time option that gets me the same result?

The degree has to fit your life—not just your LinkedIn bio.

Already in Debt? Here's What You Can Do

If you've already taken out student loans, don't panic—and don't ignore them. Here's how to take back control:

- Pay more than the minimum if you can. Even an extra $20–$50 a month can shave off months or even years.
- Know your repayment plan. Look into income-driven repayment (IDR) options—they adjust based on what you actually earn.
- Be cautious about refinancing federal loans. If you go private, you give up federal protections like Public Service Loan Forgiveness (PSLF), deferment, and income-based plans.
- Track policy changes. Student loan forgiveness isn't guaranteed, but it's evolving. Each administration tweaks the rules—stay informed, but don't bank your whole future on it.
- Don't let loans go dark. Missed payments tank your credit. If you're struggling, call your servicer and ask questions. Stay proactive. This isn't a set-it-and-forget-it situation.

You don't have to love your loans—but you do have to manage them.

Keep them in your awareness.

The Case for Forgiveness

Student loan forgiveness isn't about rewarding poor planning. It's about correcting policy failure.

Public colleges used to be funded as public goods—especially in the 1960s and early 1970s, when states covered most of the cost. That began to change in the late '70s and '80s, when tax cuts and budget shifts—led in part by Ronald Reagan, both as California governor and later as president—reduced public investment in higher education.

As funding declined, tuition rose. And instead of expanding grants, we leaned harder on student loans to fill the gap. Borrowers weren't reckless—they were navigating a system that had quietly offloaded the cost of education onto individuals.

Today, millions of borrowers—most of whom did the "right" thing—are stuck paying off debt simply because their education was shifted from public investment to private risk.

These aren't reckless spenders. They're teachers, nurses, social workers, public servants. Getting them out from under this burden doesn't just help them—it helps all of us. It increases spending power, boosts economic growth, and stabilizes communities. We saw it during the pandemic. When student loan payments paused, people had more money for housing, food, and family.

Forgiveness isn't about a handout. It's about acknowledging that the system changed—and people shouldn't have to suffer for doing what they were told was smart.

Final Thoughts: Make School Work for You

College isn't a scam. But the way we've priced it? The way we've marketed it? The way we've normalized debt as the cost of ambition?
That part absolutely is.

You don't need to graduate from a big-name school to succeed. You don't need to chase prestige to prove your worth.
What you need is a plan that works for your life—and your budget.

That might mean:

- Starting at a community college
- Skipping a for-profit program that feels like a shortcut
- Choosing a public university with solid outcomes
- Or turning down a "dream school" that only leads to debt

Education is a powerful tool—but it should build your future, not break your finances.

Don't borrow for identity. Don't mistake marketing for value. And don't wait for the system to fix itself. Navigate it wisely. Ask harder questions. Make it work for you.

Because the smartest path isn't the most expensive.
It's the one that lets you move forward—without looking back in regret.

Chapter 9: The Debt Exit Plan

A re you carrying debt that feels like it's weighing you down? Not just financially—but emotionally, mentally, even physically? Debt has a way of living rent-free in your mind while charging interest on your peace.

But here's the truth: you can break free. Not by chasing more income, but by learning how to need less.

Because that's the real lever in this system. Not just working harder—but spending with precision.

Every dollar you don't owe is a dollar you can use.

Every cost you cut is a piece of your power coming back.

With the right understanding, discipline, and a mindset shift, you can turn the weight of debt into a stepping stone.

Some debts deserve urgency. Others can be managed strategically. But none of them are unbeatable—especially when you're armed with the truth about how they work… and how spending smarter can set you free.

Ranking Debt from Worst to Least Harmful

Not all debt is created equal. Some drains your bank account slowly. Others are ticking bombs you didn't even know you lit.

Debt doesn't just drain your bank account—it rents space in your decisions. Every type has its own way of making you hesitate, compromise, or delay your goals.

In my experience, here's how I rank debts from most dangerous to least harmful—based not just on the numbers, but on how they erode your daily spend power:

1. Payday loans
2. Credit cards
3. Buy Now, Pay Later (BNPL) loans
4. Personal loans
5. Car loans
6. Student loans
7. Mortgages

Why this order? It's not just about interest rates. It's about how quickly each one eats into your freedom.

Payday loans stack interest faster than most people can breathe. Credit cards quietly rack up compounding costs while you think you're "managing." Even mortgages—often seen as wise —can eat hundreds of thousands in long-term interest.

The pattern is simple: The more it limits your options, the more dangerous it becomes.

Let's break them down—one spend trap at a time.

Payday Loans: The Ultimate Trap

This isn't just debt—it's financial quicksand.

Payday loans are structured to keep you trapped. They often market themselves as small, short-term fixes—$300 here, $500 there. But behind the friendly storefront is an industry built on predatory math. Many of these loans carry effective APRs over 400%, with compounding that hits weekly. You don't just fall behind—you sink.
Even when I was broke, I stayed away from payday loans. That wasn't luck—it was because I had someone I could call. Not

everyone does. That's the trap: these loans don't target the careless. They target the desperate.

Here's where community matters. A friend lending you $100, a family member spotting groceries, or a local credit union offering a small hardship loan can be the difference between survival and financial freefall. That's why payday lenders thrive where community ties are thin. The weaker our safety nets—public and personal—the stronger their grip.

If you're in one now, the best thing you can do is get out, even if it means asking for help (see Chapter 10). If you're considering one, stop and pause—because that moment of panic could become years of financial delay.

These loans aren't small. They're quicksand in disguise—easy to step into, almost impossible to escape.

Avoid them at all costs.

Credit Cards: Useful but Deadly

Used correctly, they can help you build credit, earn rewards, and track spending. But the second you carry a balance? They turn into one of the most expensive forms of debt on the market. That's no accident—it's by design, meant to make you overspend.
Low minimum payments, teaser rates, "rewards" that nudge you into buying more—it's a marketing ecosystem wrapped in a financial trap.

As of early 2025, the average American carries nearly $6,500 in credit card debt. That's not poor planning. It's the cost of trying to keep up—while the system quietly sells you more lifestyle than you can afford.

Let's talk numbers:

- 30% interest on $6,500 = $1,950 a year
- That's $4,000 gone every two years
- If you only make minimum payments—say $130/month —you'll be in debt for over 20 years
- By the end, you'll have paid back more than double what you borrowed

This isn't about guilt—it's about math. That's why credit card debt should be your first priority to eliminate.

Rule #1: If you can't pay it off in full, stop adding more debt.

Rule #2: Make a clear plan to knock it out.

Here's how:

- Mathematically: Use the avalanche method—pay off the card with the highest interest rate first.
- Emotionally: Use the snowball method—pay off the smallest balance first to build momentum.

Example:

If you have a $500 card at 26%, a $3,000 personal loan at 12%, and a $12,000 student loan at 6%:

- Both methods would start with the credit card—because it's both the highest interest and the smallest balance.
- After that, avalanche would move to the 12% loan. Snowball would go by smallest size.

The best method? The one you'll actually follow.

Because credit card debt isn't just expensive—it's emotionally heavy. It lingers. It nags. It whispers you're behind.

But paying it off—especially aggressively—is one of the fastest ways to free up your daily spend, reduce stress, and gain real financial breathing room.

You don't have to do it in isolation. Debt feels heavier when it's silent. Whether it's a credit-counseling group, a church circle that helps members restructure bills, or even just a friend checking in on your payoff progress, accountability turns shame into momentum. Alone, it feels endless. Together, it feels possible.

Start there. Stay focused. The goal isn't perfection—it's power.

Buy Now, Pay Later: The Silent Creep

BNPL looks harmless. It isn't.

"Four easy payments of $24.99." That's the hook. It makes a $100 impulse buy feel like a $25 decision. If that were the only thing you split into payments? Maybe it would be fine.

But that's not how BNPL works in real life. It stacks—quietly, invisibly. One item becomes four payments. Four items become sixteen. Suddenly, your passive spend is full of future charges you casually signed up for—without a full view of how they add up.

That's the silent danger of BNPL: it doesn't just spread payments—it spreads spending.
With no interest upfront, people often mistake it for "free money." But the fine print is always there, waiting. Late fees. Account holds. Credit reporting. Once you miss a payment, the friendly installment plan becomes a real financial threat.

If you use BNPL:

- Only do it for purchases you've already budgeted for in full
- Set calendar reminders for each payment
- Track your open plans manually—because the providers don't always make it obvious

If you're running multiple BNPL charges through your credit card, you've expanded your exposure. You're not avoiding debt —you're just rescheduling it.

Breakout: BNPL vs. Credit Cards – What's the Difference?

	BNPL (Buy Now, Pay Later)	**Credit Cards**
Interest	Often 0% (if paid on time)	20–30%+ if not paid in full
Due Dates	Fixed, staggered (e.g. every 2 weeks or monthly)	Rolling monthly billing cycle
Where It Hits	Sometimes your bank account... but often your credit card	Directly on your credit card
Stacking Risk	Easy to pile multiple plans without seeing the total impact	Easy to carry a balance without urgency
Mental Trap	Feels "cheap" because it's broken into parts	Feels "normal" but silently builds interest
Smart Use Case	Only if you have the full amount saved *and* a calendar system in place. Otherwise, it's just debt in disguise.	

Caution: If you're using BNPL to "float" a charge on your credit card, ask yourself—are you solving a timing issue…
or just avoiding the reality of cost?

I've used BNPL before to stagger a necessary purchase—not because I couldn't afford it, but because I had a plan, a payment schedule, and the full amount already in savings or to fit within my active spend.
But I also have a personal rule: Do not carry more than one or two BNPL plans at a time.

More than that? It's no longer cash flow—it's chaos… like trying to remember how many streaming subscriptions you have going.

Bottom Line:

- BNPL feels less serious—but that's what makes it dangerous
- Credit cards feel manageable—but the interest adds up fast
- Neither is "bad" on its own—the trap is in overuse, not awareness

Personal Loans: Friend or Foe

Personal loans sit in a weird middle space: they're not inherently dangerous, but they can quietly reinforce the same bad habits that got you into debt in the first place.

Used strategically, they can absolutely help. Especially if you're consolidating higher-interest credit card debt into a lower fixed rate, they might save you thousands in interest over time.

Example: $6,500 in credit card debt at 24% could cost over $1,500 a year in interest.
A 4-year personal loan at 11.5% cuts that nearly in half.

That's real money. But here's the trap:

A personal loan isn't progress if your spending hasn't changed.
You didn't solve the problem—you just reset the clock.

This is the passive spending danger most people don't see. A
personal loan lowers your monthly burden, but if you're still
spending the same amount on restaurants, gadgets, or random
Amazon hauls? You're not gaining ground. You're just
repackaging the damage.

Because personal loans are often used during financial stress—
medical bills, emergencies, unexpected repairs—it's easy to
think of them as survival tools. Even in those moments, you
have to be ruthless about what you can afford to pay back
monthly.

Sometimes the smartest move isn't another loan at all—it's
asking for help first. A landlord might allow a one-month
extension. A sibling might cover part of a bill. A local nonprofit
might step in with food or utility assistance so you can redirect
cash to urgent payments. Those options aren't weakness—
they're survival strategies that keep you from compounding the
problem.

If the payment stretches you thin, it's not a solution. It's just
quieter chaos.

The bottom line: A personal loan can help reduce interest—but
it can't fix overspending.
Only needing less can do that.

Car Loans: The Overlooked Drain

Car loans don't get enough scrutiny—probably because they're
so common. But just because something is "normal" doesn't
mean it's financially healthy.

Cars lose value the second you drive them off the lot. So when you borrow money to buy one, you're paying interest on something that's losing value every single day.
That's a double loss.

Yet car loans often get a pass because they don't feel dangerous. They're not marketed like credit cards. You don't swipe them at checkout. But over time? A car loan can quietly eat away your financial flexibility.

If you're spending $600 a month on a car payment—and another $150 on insurance—you're looking at nearly $9,000 a year just to keep it on the road.
That's not transportation. That's a lifestyle cost.

Here's how to keep it in check:

- Keep the loan term under five years. Anything longer is just financial bait. A 7-year loan might lower your monthly payment—but it raises the total cost, leaves you upside down longer, and locks you into a car that's losing value the entire time.
- Shop rates with credit unions and online lenders, not just the dealer. Dealers often inflate the rate to pad their profit.
- Buy used whenever possible. A two-year-old model could save you thousands upfront and reduce your insurance costs.

Here's a little-known truth:
If you're pre-approved for a car loan through a bank or credit union, you often don't need to put any money down.
That's not advice to skip the down payment—but it's a reminder that dealers often push for it to protect themselves, not you.

A pre-approval is like cash. The loan is the offer. The down payment? That's a negotiation tactic, not a rule.

If the monthly payment locks you out of saving, traveling, or breathing financially, it's not freedom—it's a financial leash. Yes, cars can be necessary. But let's be real: in many cases, people are financing the car they want instead of the one they need. That's how a $25,000 car becomes a $40,000 mistake.

If the only way you can "afford" the car is to stretch the loan to seven years? You can't afford the car.

Don't borrow for image. Borrow for function—and only if your budget can actually carry it.

Student Loans: Strategic Repayment

Student loans aren't evil—but they're absolutely dangerous if you treat them casually.

Unlike credit cards or BNPL, student debt often doesn't feel urgent. The payments are smaller. The interest rates are lower. You might get a grace period.
That's exactly what makes it risky—it hides.

It sits in the background while you chase your first job, your first apartment, your first life. Then one day you look up and realize the balance hasn't moved much—because most of your payments have been going to interest, not principal.

Here's what matters most: pay early, pay aggressively. The sooner you chip away at the principal, the less you'll spend overall. Student loan interest may look small on paper—but over ten or twenty years, it adds up fast.

If you're paying $300 a month, but only $80 goes to the actual loan? You're not reducing your debt—you're just renting it.

I was able to deduct a large portion of my MBA tuition—legally —because I was working in a related role while studying, and the degree directly advanced my existing career. I even had to prove that twice—to two different IRS agents. But because I had clear records and a real connection between the job and the degree, it held up both times.

The point isn't to copy that strategy—it's to show that if your education ties directly to your job, and if you're careful and well-documented, there may be ways to lessen the burden. But that's a conversation to have with a real tax professional—not a book, not a website, and definitely not your cousin who "does taxes on the side."

What about forgiveness? Assume nothing. Unless you're already in a federal loan forgiveness program and meeting every requirement precisely, you need to act as if it's on you. That may sound harsh, but it's the most financially responsible stance.

Hope for relief, but plan for none.

Student loans are often unavoidable. But if you treat them passively, you'll pay for them twice: once with your money, and once with your freedom.

Mortgages: Necessary Evil, Manage Wisely

Mortgages carry a myth—one of the biggest in personal finance. The idea that buying a home is automatically a good investment. That it's the key to building wealth. That it's the American Dream.

But here's the truth: a mortgage is just a loan tied to a depreciating structure.
Yes, real estate can appreciate—but the house itself? It ages. It breaks. It costs.

A $400,000 mortgage over 30 years at 6.5% interest will cost you over $900,000 in total payments by the time it's s done—and that's not counting repairs, property taxes, or maintenance—just the loan. That's not equity. That's expense.

Can buying a home be the right move? Of course. But it's not inherently smart. It's only smart if:

- You stay long enough to outpace transaction costs
- You can comfortably afford the monthly payment and the hidden upkeep
- You're not draining your cash reserves to force it

Renting doesn't mean you're "throwing money away." You're paying for flexibility. You're avoiding debt. You're buying time. That's not wasteful—it's strategic.

Don't fall for the "house hacking" hype if the math doesn't work. Renting out rooms or buying with friends can help, but it also adds pressure and risk. If you can't afford the house on your own, you can't afford it. Period.

Also be wary of refinancing traps. Refinancing can make sense if:

- You're significantly lowering your interest rate
- You're shortening your loan term without extending debt
- The fees don't erase the gains

But refinancing just to lower your monthly payment—by stretching your loan out another 30 years? That's a step backward. Not forward.

If you're considering a mortgage, run the numbers honestly. Look at total cost, not just the monthly bite. Understand that buying a home may mean:

- You can't take a new job across the country
- You have to pay $15,000 for a roof you weren't expecting
- You're committed to a neighborhood that may change faster than your finances

Owning a home isn't the finish line. It's just a very expensive starting point.

If you're not ready, renting isn't failure—it's freedom. If the juice isn't worth the squeeze, pass.

Debt is the Shadow of Past Spending

Every dollar of debt is a reflection of a past spend. That's not a moral failure—it's just a fact. You already spent the money. Now it's about reclaiming control.

You don't need to carry shame—but you do need to know the cause. Was it an emergency? Lifestyle creep? Emotional spending? Name it. Learn from it. That's how you make sure you don't end up back in the same place.

Here's what no one tells you: you're going to mess up again. You'll overspend. You'll panic. You'll miss a payment. Don't overcorrect. Don't crash your whole budget trying to make up for one mistake. Like driving, it's safer to reroute calmly than swerve across lanes.

You're not broken because you took on debt. You were surviving. Now, you're building. Every payment is a step back toward control, dignity, and peace.

Remember: building rarely happens alone. A neighbor splitting costs, a friend offering a ride instead of you financing another car, a public library saving you from a subscription—you gain ground faster when you plug into community. Every shared resource lightens the load, which makes your exit plan sturdier.

You don't have to be perfect—you just have to keep showing up.

- Stop adding to the pile.
- Pay off aggressively where you can.
- Spend forward with purpose, not pressure.

Debt doesn't own you anymore. You do.

In the next chapter, we'll lay out exactly how to protect your money—and your momentum—as you rebuild.

Chapter 10: Asking for Help Isn't Weakness

How often do you feel alone while in your finances? Most people do. And it's not because they're bad with money—it's because they've been left to figure it out alone. We're handed a debit card at 18, a credit card a few years later, and then expected to manage everything from rent to retirement without ever being taught how.

When it gets hard—and it will get hard—we're taught to hide it. To internalize the pressure. To assume that needing help means we failed. That silence is strength. That shame is justified.

But none of that's true.

This stigma around asking for help isn't an accident. It's been built—brick by brick, message by message—for decades. You've been told that taxes are theft, that government programs are handouts, and that anyone who accepts public support is taking advantage of the system. Meanwhile, the wealthiest Americans are quietly cashing in on tax breaks, credits, and legal loopholes designed just for them.

You've been told to hate the IRS… but the real problem is the people rewriting the rules. The wealthy donors, lobbyists, and elected officials who've redirected public wealth for private gain—while convincing you that the safety net is the enemy.

This isn't new. The East India Company cut sweetheart deals with governments centuries ago. Today, Silicon Valley's tech giants do the same with cities—promising jobs, demanding tax breaks, and leaving the local population footing the bill. Yet, while billion-dollar corporations are subsidized without shame, a parent is ridiculed for using SNAP benefits to feed their child—just trying to keep them alive today so they can promise some kind of future tomorrow.

That double standard is the point: corporate self-interest is celebrated, but personal survival is stigmatized.

Here's the truth: every time you don't use a program you qualify for, the system saves money. Every time you're too embarrassed to ask for help, the cycle continues. Every time you pay interest on debt instead of applying for aid, someone else profits from your silence.

This isn't just about personal pride. It's about structural manipulation. Because when people don't ask for help, they spend more. The longer they struggle alone, the harder it is to catch up. That's the real trap. Not the spending itself—but the isolation that comes with it.

Needing less is a form of power. But needing help is not a weakness.

If asking for support helps you avoid debt, regain momentum, or stop financial free fall… that's not dependence. That's strategy. That's choosing a better path instead of sinking deeper into a broken one.

Asking for help is a financial decision. In many cases, it's the smartest one you can make.

The Moment I Asked for Help

I've never forgotten the day I called my mom to say I was drowning. Not because I didn't know how to budget—but because for the first time, my system cracked under pressure.

I had just moved to Atlanta. New job. New rent. A car payment. Furniture I had to finance. Passive expenses were stacking faster than I could manage, and despite years of financial discipline, my credit card balance hit $6,000. That number—six thousand—felt like failure. But it wasn't. It was a flare. A warning that something needed to change.

And that change started with help.

I didn't just ask my mom for money—I showed her my plan. I had built a spreadsheet. I was splitting rent across the month to make it manageable. I was living on $8 a day and ordering off the dollar menu. I wasn't panicking—I was rebuilding.

She saw that. Then she stepped in.
She lent me the $6,000—not as a bailout, but as a bridge. That loan became the first true partnership in my financial life. From that day forward, she helped me challenge every assumption. Why spend this? Why not wait? What's the daily impact of that monthly decision?

Her support bought me more than breathing room. It gave me clarity. It gave me a second chance at discipline. It helped me rebuild a system that would later become the foundation of this book.

It also taught me something critical: asking for help early prevents the spiral. When you catch it before it becomes survival mode, you can act with strategy—not panic.

You don't need to reach a breaking point to ask for support. You just need the humility to say, "This is starting to slip—and I don't want it to get worse."

Friends & Family: No More Secrets

Some of the worst financial stress comes not from the numbers —but from the silence around them. And I've seen that silence wreck friendships, drain bank accounts, and leave people ashamed for no reason at all.

When I lived in Atlanta, I had a group of friends with wildly different incomes. Some made $35,000. Others made over $150,000. But you wouldn't have known it—because no one talked about money. People skipped events without saying why.

Others stretched themselves too thin trying to keep up. It was a social performance… and it was costing us.

That's the hidden tax of secrecy. When you don't talk about income, or rent, or debt, you make isolation the norm. When isolation sets in, people make worse decisions. They overspend to keep up. They ghost friends when they can't afford plans. They carry financial shame that could be softened with a single honest conversation.

Transparency isn't just a virtue—it's a tactic. Talk openly with the people you trust. Ask how much they spend on things. Share what you're working on financially. If you can say, "Hey, I'm budgeting this month," it opens the door for better decisions across the board—group dinners become potlucks, weekends get cheaper, and nobody feels like they're faking it just to belong.

And when it comes to housing? Living alone might feel like success, but it can quietly wreck your budget. I've long had a personal rule: if rent or mortgage is over $1,000 a month, I seriously consider getting a roommate. It's not regression—it's leverage. Every dollar you save now is freedom later.

We have to stop pretending that struggling is rare. It's not. What's rare is the courage to say it out loud.

Family Support: With Respect and Structure

Family help can be messy. It can also be transformative. The key is structure.

Before I started my MBA in 2015, I sat down with my mom and mapped out what support might look like. We didn't just wing it. We planned. We agreed she'd help under the annual IRS gift exclusion—$14,000 at the time, now $19,000 in 2025. That kept it clean. Legal. Simple. No weird IOUs or unspoken pressure.

And that support didn't just keep me from taking out loans. It kept me from spending the next decade repaying them. We eliminated over $120,000 in student debt before it even had a chance to grow. That changed everything—from the jobs I could take to the city I could live in. My financial future wasn't just less stressful. It was flexible.

But the only reason it worked was because we treated it like a partnership, not a rescue. There were boundaries, clarity, and mutual respect.

You don't need generational wealth to build something like this. You just need:

- Honesty about what's possible
- A clear plan for how the support will be used
- A shared understanding of what comes next

If you're the one offering help to a family member, the same rules apply. Don't give more than you can afford to. Don't say yes just to avoid guilt. And if you do give—give with a full heart or not at all.

Because money isn't just a resource. It's a relationship. And how you give or receive it can either build trust… or quietly destroy it.

Structuring Help to Protect Relationships

Money is one of the fastest ways to erode trust. Not because people are greedy—but because expectations are rarely clear. If you're going to borrow from someone—or help someone financially—you need more than good intentions. You need structure.

If you're asking for help:

- Be direct about what you need, and why.
- Offer a timeline for repayment if it's a loan—not just "when I can."
- Put it in writing, even if it's informal. Not because you expect drama—but because structure prevents it.
- Keep them in the loop. Update them without being prompted. Show that their trust isn't being taken for granted.

And if you're the one giving:

- Be clear about your boundaries. What can you give without resentment?
- Decide up front: is this a gift or a loan?
- Don't let guilt drive your decision. Help should come from care, not pressure.
- Know your limits. If giving jeopardizes your own stability, it's not sustainable.

You're not just protecting your wallet—you're protecting the relationship. That relationship might matter more than the money ever will.

Because at its core, asking for help isn't about desperation—it's about connection. And how you set that up determines whether it becomes a lifeline… or a landmine.

Dating & Finances: Talk About It Early

Money is the second most common reason relationships end—right after cheating. That stat isn't just trivia. It's a warning.

If you want a financially healthy relationship, you have to talk about money early and honestly. Before you move in together. Before you combine anything. Before the resentment sets in.

For me, I usually pay for the first few dates. It's not about gender roles or impressing anyone—it's my choice. But after that, I shift toward proportional sharing. Not 50/50... fair.

Let's say one person makes $40,000 and the other makes $60,000. That's a 40/60 split. If rent is $2,000, one person pays $800 and the other pays $1,200. That's not just math—it's a mindset shift. It says: "We both contribute. We both carry what we can."

It should extend beyond rent, too. Shared dinners, vacations, utilities—it all works better when expectations are clear. Because nothing builds quiet resentment faster than feeling like you're subsidizing someone who won't acknowledge it.

It also means avoiding social spending traps. If one of you wants to go out for sushi and the other is trying to save, talk about it. Choose a cheaper spot. Rotate who picks. Be flexible. Financial health in a relationship comes from adaptability, not perfection.

And for the love of all things holy... don't pull the "group check" move where you order the lobster and then expect to split the bill evenly. Respect people's budgets. Ask what works. Be kind—and direct.

Money doesn't ruin relationships. Silence does.

Government Help: You're Entitled to It — Use It

There is a myth in America that needing help means you failed. That if you ask for assistance, you're weak. That programs like food aid, rent support, or healthcare are somehow a handout.

That's not just wrong—it's propaganda. And it's expensive propaganda, too.

Because here's the truth: if you make under half a million dollars a year—and especially if you're under $100K—there are programs that exist for you. They are not favors. They are entitlements. That means you qualify for them by law. You paid taxes. Your neighbors did too. These programs are the return on that investment.

And yet millions of people never apply. Not because they're too proud—but because the process was designed to wear them down.

Applications are long. Phone calls are dropped. Offices are understaffed. People give up, or feel embarrassed, or never even know what they're eligible for. That's not a bug in the system. That is the system.

But here's the part no one tells you: borrowing money you can't afford to repay is not more honorable than accepting help you already qualify for. Refusing assistance while quietly drowning in debt doesn't make you stronger—it just delays your recovery. There are programs worth exploring:

- SNAP (food support for working families)
- WIC (assistance for pregnant people and young children)
- Medicaid (healthcare for low-income or disabled individuals)
- Section 8 (rent support for qualified tenants)
- LIHEAP (help with utility bills)
- Pell Grants (tuition assistance)
- CalFresh (California-specific food aid)

These aren't hypothetical. They change lives:

- A mom in Fresno feeds her kids because of WIC.
- A college student in Ohio earns a degree with zero debt thanks to Pell Grants.
- A diabetic man in Arkansas stops rationing insulin thanks to Medicaid.
- A veteran in San Diego stays housed through Section 8.

If you qualify and don't apply, that's money left on the table. That's cash you're already owed... and choosing not to claim it helps no one.

So take the help. Document everything. And when the application makes you feel like a burden? Remember: the real burden is pretending you don't need support when you do.

Because this isn't about pride. It's about math.

What Stops Us from Asking for Help?

If support is available—and if you qualify for it—then why do so many people never ask?

The answer runs deeper than numbers. It's not just about eligibility. It's about pride, fear, trauma, and shame. For some, especially men, asking for help feels like failure. Like surrendering your identity. For others, especially in communities of color, asking for help has often meant being ignored, judged, or penalized. There's a long, painful history there—and it doesn't fade just because the form is online now.

And then there's the system itself. Even when we do ask, we're often met with confusing forms, long waits, and rejection letters that feel like punishment. The very act of applying can feel like an obstacle course built to weed people out.

But the truth is this: not asking has a cost, too. It leads to debt that lingers. Credit cards that never get paid off. Medical bills that balloon. And slowly, your future options shrink.

That's why this chapter matters. Because whether you're asking a parent, a friend, or the government—you're not just asking for money. You're asking for a lifeline. A reset. A chance to breathe again.

The hardest part isn't applying. It's believing you're worth the support.

You are.

When Help Fails You

Sometimes, even when you do everything right—ask with humility, explain your situation, show the math—the answer is still no.

Maybe a friend says they can't lend the money.
Maybe your family brushes it off or makes it emotional.
Maybe the government sends a rejection letter that feels robotic and cold.

That moment hurts. Not just because you're still in need… but because rejection in a vulnerable moment feels like confirmation that you're on your own.

But here's what's true, even if it doesn't feel true in the moment: not all help comes from the first place you look. Not all "no's" are final.

Rejection doesn't mean you were wrong to ask. It means this version of the plan didn't work.

That's why your strategy has to go deeper than hope. If Plan A fails, you build Plan B with whatever is in reach. You pivot. You adjust. You keep your dignity.

Financial shame thrives in silence—but persistence is louder. There is power in continuing to ask, to try again, to find a path through.

Because sometimes the breakthrough isn't who says yes. It's that you kept going after someone said no.

The Financial Power of Asking

Let's make one thing clear: asking for help isn't just emotional. It's financial.

When you ask for help, you're not giving up control—you're buying it back. You're shrinking your debt timeline. You're preventing a cascade of interest, fees, and stress. You're choosing recovery over pride.

And in real numbers? That matters.

Asking your landlord for a short extension can save a late fee. Calling your credit card company might lower your APR. Using a food assistance program could free up $300/month for other essentials.
Borrowing from a trusted family member—even just once— could eliminate years of compound interest.

The system is built to make you feel like you have to go it alone. But almost no one who's thriving financially is actually doing it solo. They're using every tool available—family help, tax advantages, public programs, strategic borrowing. Not because they're desperate. Because they're smart.

When I asked my mom for help? It wasn't weakness—it was leverage.

When I started sharing money conversations with friends? It wasn't awkward—it was freedom.

When I used public support to avoid a deeper financial spiral? That wasn't shameful—it was survival.

So ask yourself:

- Who do you trust enough to talk to?
- What aid exists that you haven't tapped into?
- Where is your pride costing you more than your debt?

Because asking is part of the plan. It's not a detour. It's a tool. In a system where the costs never stop, needing less—and getting support when you need it—is the smartest financial move you can make.

Chapter 11: The Redistribution of Theft

Y ou might think your Netflix auto-renewal or unused gym membership is the sneakiest kind of passive spending—but there's something even more invisible. Something that disappears before you ever touch it. You don't swipe a card. You don't approve the charge. You just... lose it. Every paycheck. Every year. Without question.

We're talking about taxes.

I know—this isn't the fun part. But skipping this chapter would be like skipping rent in your budget breakdown. You can't afford to. Because for many Americans, taxes are one of the top three passive expenses in life—up there with housing and healthcare. But unlike rent or groceries, taxes don't feel like a decision. You can't negotiate your bracket. You can't call and cancel.

So we treat it like a loss. Like theft. Like something done to us rather than for us.

But here's the truth: you already paid. You already contributed. You built roads. You funded schools. You helped veterans, supported disaster relief, and stocked emergency rooms.

Taxes are not the enemy. Misdirection is.

This isn't a new problem. Over a century ago, during America's first Gilded Age, wealth pooled at the top while workers carried the load. We're watching the sequel play out now—a second Gilded Age where money moves upward quietly, one tax cut, one loophole, one missed public investment at a time. Misdirection works best when you're exhausted. When the system makes you feel powerless, confused, or cynical—like nothing you do matters. That's by design. Because the more checked out we are, the easier it is for powerful interests to quietly steer our public money into private pockets.

But it doesn't have to be that way.

In Germany, you can log into a government portal and see where your taxes went. In Canada, your healthcare bill isn't a panic attack—it's a reminder that public systems can actually work. In the Netherlands, childcare is publicly subsidized and affordable. These aren't fantasies. They're policy choices—proof that government can make life easier… if we demand it.

So no, this chapter isn't about tax loopholes or filing hacks. It's about reclaiming something bigger: your share of the country you're already paying for. Because until we treat taxes as spending we control, we'll keep letting others spend it for us.

Let's dig in.

The Flow of Money Matters

Once upon a time, someone had a simple idea:
Economies grow stronger when the people at the bottom have more money.

Not the billionaires. Not the banks.
But the people who fix the cars, stock the shelves, run the classrooms, and hold the economy together one paycheck at a time.

When you give them money, they spend it—on groceries, on gas, on rent, on life.
That spending moves. It circulates. It keeps others employed.

That's how a healthy economy works: money moves.
It doesn't sit in savings accounts or stock portfolios.
It flows. And every time it moves, it helps someone else.

So maybe the real question isn't how much the rich have.
Maybe it's: how fast is money moving… and who gets to move it?

Where Does It Even Go?

Ever wonder where your tax dollars actually end up?

Here's a breakdown of how the average U.S. taxpayer's federal income taxes were spent in 2023, according to the National Priorities Project:

- Health Programs: $5,243 went to Medicare, Medicaid, and public health.
- Military and Defense: $5,110 funded weapons, bases, and global operations.
- Interest on National Debt: $3,187 just to service what we already owe.
- Unemployment and Labor: $1,429 for job support and benefits.
- Education: $1,898 for public schools, special education, and college aid.
- Food and Agriculture: $668 for programs like SNAP and school lunches.
- Transportation: $526 for roads, bridges, and public transit.
- Veterans Benefits: $805 for healthcare, housing, and support services.
- Everything Else: $733 to cover housing, disaster response, environmental protection, and more.

That's your money. Not a suggestion. Not a GoFundMe. A mandatory contribution you've already made—every month, every year, whether you benefit or not.

When you zoom out, taxes aren't just a line on your paycheck. They're a declaration of what we prioritize… or pretend to.

So ask yourself: does this breakdown match the life you're living?

Because the answer for most people is: not even close.

You've heard the slogans—"Support our troops," "Back the blue," "Protect our kids." But did you know that one in four active-duty military families faces food insecurity? Or that thousands of teachers in the U.S. work second jobs just to survive? Or that hospital wait times have surged in rural towns while defense contractors rake in record profits?

It's not that we don't fund these systems. It's that we don't fund the people inside them.

Take the F-35 fighter jet. It was supposed to be the crown jewel of U.S. airpower. Instead, it became a monument to corporate overreach. Originally priced under $200 billion, it's now projected to cost over $2 trillion in total. That's more than the GDP of Canada. And yet it still can't safely fly through a thunderstorm.

Meanwhile, in Finland, public school teachers are paid well, respected as experts, and given time to collaborate. In Sweden, clean drinking water isn't a privilege—it's a baseline. In Australia, prescription drugs are capped so no one chooses between insulin and rent.
Those countries didn't spend less. They just spent better.

We could have universal pre-K. Debt-free community college. Nationwide broadband. Climate-resilient infrastructure. School lunch for every child, every day.

You already paid for all of it. The question is: who stole the return?

This is why so many Americans feel like the government is broken. Because we fund it like a modern country, but it often functions like a failing one. Not because public programs don't work—but because we stopped demanding they work for us.

That can change. But only if we treat this like what it is: not charity... not policy... but spending. Yours.

Why Government Spending Feels Broken (And How to Fix It)

Let's get one thing straight: the idea that government spending is mostly waste? That didn't come from some diligent public audit. It came from billionaires. The same ones who lobby for tax cuts while convincing you that feeding kids or fixing bridges is somehow frivolous.

But here's the actual math. Federal spending on things like unemployment benefits, food programs, and infrastructure doesn't just circulate—it multiplies. Economists call it the multiplier effect. For every dollar spent on these programs, the economy can grow by $1.50 or more. That's not waste. That's return on investment.

The problem isn't too much spending. It's misaligned spending. Overspending in the wrong places. Underspending in the right ones. And zero clarity on how the money moves.

Which is why so many Americans are skeptical. Because even when the intent is good, the experience is opaque.

That's where reform has to start—not just in budgets, but in trust.

Imagine this. Each month, the federal government sends you an email—just like your credit card company does. It says: "Here's what your taxes funded this month." A breakdown. A visual. Maybe a comparison to last month's budget. Then, in April, you get a full Taxes Wrapped report—like Spotify Wrapped, but for your civic impact. "This year, your taxes helped fund 43 days of school lunches, repaired 600 feet of highway, and kept emergency rooms open in your region."

That's not fluff. That's ownership.

We already track our screen time, our steps, our spending. Why not our contribution to the collective good?

But don't stop at information. Pair that monthly email with tools for action.

Imagine it links you directly to your local, state, and federal reps. It shows exactly how much of your income went where— and what could've been funded instead. Not in vague terms. In cold, hard, line-item clarity.

This year, $4,312 of your paycheck went to defense contracts and debt interest. That same amount could've fully funded after-school programs in your county.

Now imagine you're not just reading it—you're running on it.

That's what real democracy looks like. A feedback loop where taxpayers don't just pay—they direct. They hold receipts. They apply pressure. They organize.

This isn't just about government reform. It's about turning data into democracy.

Because the truth is, most people don't feel disconnected from taxes because they hate public goods. They feel disconnected because there's no bridge between what they give… and what they can change.

That bridge is long overdue.

Let's build it.

What We Need Are Three Targeted Reforms:

Fixing the system doesn't require reinventing the wheel. It just means redesigning the incentives—so that public money serves the public good, not private bloat.

The first fix is simple: stop punishing government agencies for being efficient. Right now, many departments follow zero-based budgeting, which means if they're allocated $100 and only spend $95, their next year's budget drops. So what do smart teams do? They spend the full $100, whether they need to or not. The incentive is to waste—or risk getting penalized for saving money.

We need to flip that logic. Every year, Congress should hold Financial Efficiency Reviews, where departments that underspend without compromising results are asked a single question: what worked?

These aren't gold star ceremonies. They're learning sessions. If a team saved money by restructuring a contract, modernizing a process, or eliminating redundancies, that strategy should be documented and replicated. Efficiency shouldn't be a liability. It should be a playbook.

The second fix is smarter bidding on public contracts. No more open-ended price tags. If a contractor bids $100 million, then that's the limit. If they go over, they cover the difference. And if they come in under budget—let's say they deliver for $90 million—they get to keep the remaining $10 million as profit. But only if the final cost is within 90% of their original bid. That's how you encourage realistic proposals and responsible execution.

Because here's what happens now. A company bids $100 million, then ends up charging $140 million, and taxpayers eat the overage. Or they lowball the bid to win the contract, then cry poor halfway through and demand more money to finish the job. And guess what? They usually get it.

Want a real-world example? Look at California's unemployment insurance system during the pandemic. Hundreds of millions went to contractors to modernize fraud protection and handle the surge in claims. But the rollout was a disaster—over $20 billion in fraud, and real people waiting weeks for support.

Under this model, those contractors would've been on the hook. If they promised functionality and failed, they'd pay for it. If they padded their bid and still delivered garbage, no bonus. The only way to win would be to deliver the full job, at the full scope, within a reasonable margin.

That changes everything. It rewards real results—not connections, not grift, not cost overruns buried in fine print.

The third fix is about taxes themselves.

In the 1950s, the top marginal income tax rate was over 90%. That's not a typo. For today's economy, that's equivalent to taxing income over about $5 million a year at 91 to 94%. That was the era when we built highways, funded schools, and supported families on a single income. It wasn't a perfect system—but the investment in shared infrastructure paid off.

Today, we need a version of that again. Not confiscation. Contribution. People benefitting the most from the economy should be contributing the most to keep it functioning.

We need to bring back a high marginal tax rate on ultra-high incomes. But we also need something else: a 10% annual tax on assets over $10 million. And no, this isn't about your 401(k). This is about yachts, real estate portfolios, offshore trusts, and billionaires paying lower effective tax rates than their assistants.

To understand why this starts at $10 million, think about how far out of reach that really is.

If you made $100,000 a year and somehow saved every single dollar—no rent, no groceries, no taxes—it would still take you 100 years just to reach $10 million. At $1 million a year, you'd need 10 years to get there.

Now imagine earning a billion dollars. At $100,000 a year, you'd need 10,000 years—longer than recorded human history. Even at $1 million a year, it's a 1,000-year climb.
These aren't fortunes built by working harder. They're fortunes built by owning assets, leveraging capital, and benefiting from rules tilted toward the already wealthy.

Here's the kicker: research shows there's no meaningful boost in happiness beyond $10 million. In a Harvard study, people worth over $10 million reported only 0.25 points higher happiness on a 10-point scale than those worth $1–2 million. Billion-dollar wealth doesn't buy billion-dollar joy—it buys billion-dollar influence.

Federal law already draws this line. Right now, the IRS lets an individual transfer roughly $13 million tax-free over their lifetime (double that for couples) before estate and gift taxes apply. In other words, we've already said that fortunes up to this size can move across generations without penalty. A wealth tax that only kicks in above $10 million isn't radical—it's simply asking fortunes well beyond what's already tax-exempt to finally contribute back to the society that made them possible.

That's why taxing extreme wealth isn't about punishing ambition. It's about correcting a system where wealth compounds so far past the point of human benefit that it starves public goods for generations.

Let's be clear: this tax can't be sidestepped through trusts. Right now, much of America's largest fortunes are shielded inside dynasty trusts and shell entities, making billion-dollar estates look small on paper. The law must treat beneficial ownership—not just whose name is on the title—as taxable. If you control or benefit from the assets, whether directly or through a trust, it counts.

A billionaire with $1.01 billion in assets wouldn't lose their fortune overnight under this plan. Even with a 10% annual tax on wealth above $10 million, it would take more than four decades for those assets to shrink down to $10 million—without counting any new gains they'd likely make along the way. This isn't seizure. It's a deliberate, fair return of wealth that's been locked away for generations while schools, hospitals, and public infrastructure have been starved of funding.

The IRS would need the tools to pierce these layers—just like we already do to fight money laundering. Third-party reporting and modernized audits could reveal real control, making it impossible to quietly pass vast fortunes tax-free while nurses and teachers pay every dime. Trusts won't be escape hatches anymore—they'll finally contribute to the public good like everyone else.

But let's go further. If someone attempts to move assets overseas to avoid contributing their fair share, they shouldn't be rewarded for abandoning the public that built their fortune. We propose this: a 95% exit tax on any assets transferred abroad for the purpose of avoiding taxation. Call it what it is—economic desertion. You don't get to enjoy the benefits of a country—its roads, its labor, its legal protections—and then ghost when it's time to pay the bill. If you try to move $100 million out of reach? You're leaving with five.

This isn't wealth redistribution. **It's the redistribution of theft.** Because every tax cut for the rich is money taken from school lunches, clean water, public transit, and your future.

Warren Buffett once pointed out that Berkshire Hathaway paid over $5 billion in federal taxes in a single year — and that if 800 other companies had done the same, no one else in the United States would have had to pay a dime in federal taxes.

Think about that for a second. Every crumbling bridge, every overcrowded school, every underfunded hospital could be repaired not by new taxes, but by collecting what's already owed. And if the wealthiest paid their fair share alongside every working American who already does, we could start paying down the national debt and rebuilding this country from the ground up.

That's social capitalism — investing back in ourselves.

No one needs a third yacht. But your neighbor needs insulin. Your kid needs a nurse. Your street needs to be safe to walk on.

This isn't radical. It's responsible. It's how we stop bleeding cash through misaligned incentives and start funding the things that actually make life better.

But fairness doesn't stop with billionaires. It starts inside the institutions that shape our daily lives—the corporations where wealth concentrates and wages stagnate.

We've been here before. Over a century ago, during the first Gilded Age, wealth pooled at the top while workers scraped by without power or protections. Tycoons controlled entire industries, politicians bent to corporate will, and ordinary people were locked out of decisions that shaped their lives. It took decades of antitrust laws, labor reforms, and high marginal taxes to rebalance the system.

Today, history is repeating itself. Corporate power has consolidated again, wages have stagnated, and democracy has been quietly stripped from the workplace. The fix we needed then—a redistribution of power alongside wealth—is the fix we need now.

But inequality isn't sustained by billionaires alone—it's institutional. It lives inside corporate balance sheets, boardrooms, and business models that profit from dependency. That's where the next fix begins.

Corporate Power and Employee Voting Rights

When we talk about corporate taxation, it's easy to imagine the solution is just to "tax the rich more." But we've tried tweaks and loophole patches for decades, and little has changed. Wealth keeps concentrating at the top because corporate power is designed to flow upward, not outward.

Here's the missing piece: real democracy doesn't stop at the ballot box—it extends into the workplace.

Some companies already understand this.
Dr. Bronner's—the California–based soap company—caps its executive pay at no more than five times the salary of its lowest-paid employee. Their CEO earns around $300,000 a year in a company where entry-level workers make a living wage with full benefits. The result? Low turnover, steady growth, and zero dependence on taxpayer-funded welfare. That's not radical—that's responsible capitalism.

Under the model I'm proposing, that structure wouldn't be a feel-good anomaly—it would be the baseline.

The corporate tax rate would default to 25%, with a 40% penalty rate applied to any company that fails to meet four fairness standards that prioritize workers over stockholders:

1. Pay Ratio Rule: The total compensation of the highest-paid executive—including bonuses, stock options, and deferred pay—cannot exceed five times the salary of the lowest-paid full-time employee.

2. Workforce Welfare Rule: If more than 5% of a company's total workforce—including part-time, seasonal, and contract workers—relies on public assistance such as SNAP, Medicaid, or housing subsidies, that company is automatically moved to the 40% rate until it raises wages enough to eliminate that dependency.

3. Voting Rights Rule: All employee shareholders—those receiving equity as part of compensation, profit-sharing, or retirement programs—must receive equal voting rights per share as executives and institutional investors. Ownership must mean power, not symbolism.

4. Stock Buyback Ban: Companies may not repurchase their own stock to inflate share prices or executive bonuses. Profits must instead be reinvested into wages, research, sustainability, or long-term growth.

And there's one more non-negotiable: no more deductions, shelters, or zero-tax accounting tricks.

If a corporation generates profit inside the United States, it pays its share—period. No offshore subsidiaries, no deferred credits, no paper losses offsetting record revenue. Amazon shouldn't pay zero dollars in federal tax while using public roads, public airspace, and a public workforce.

These reforms would rebalance corporate power from the inside out.

Right now, executives can green-light layoffs, suppress wages, or funnel billions into buybacks without resistance from the very people who make the company valuable. Workers may hold tiny slivers of stock through retirement plans, but they have no real say. They're investors in name only.

When employees have equal voting shares, that changes everything.
Suddenly, decisions about executive pay, layoffs, and long-term direction require consideration from the workforce itself.
Leadership becomes accountable not just to Wall Street, but to the people whose lives and labor actually sustain the business.

This isn't about punishing success or strangling innovation. It's about aligning incentives. A healthy economy doesn't need billionaires hoarding capital. It needs entrepreneurs, small-business owners, and employees who can afford to take risks, start ventures, and innovate without living paycheck to paycheck.

Corporate democracy doesn't kill ambition—it multiplies it.

When workers have equity, stability, and power, they don't just survive—they create.
True innovation doesn't come from inflated share prices—it comes from people with breathing room and a stake in what they build.

Because a company that depends on taxpayer-funded welfare to sustain its workforce or manipulates its own stock to enrich executives isn't efficient—it's parasitic.
And the tax code should stop rewarding the infection.

The Debt We Don't Talk About

Every time someone says "we can't afford it," you should ask: can't afford it… or won't pay for it?

Because the truth is, we already spent it. The debt is already on the books. And the reason it's there isn't because of some out-of-control grocery list of public programs—it's because of decades of tax cuts and giveaways to the people least in need of help.

Right now, the U.S. national debt is over $34 trillion. That number gets tossed around like a threat. Like it's your fault. Like it means we need to gut healthcare, defund education, and "tighten belts" across the board.

But it's not abstract when you look at where that money is going. Interest payments on the debt are now one of the largest single lines in the federal budget. We're spending more just to keep the debt alive than we are on some entire departments.

And no, it's not because of food stamps or school meals or Section 8. That's the bait and switch. Social programs are rarely the problem—they often pay for themselves through long-term improvements in health, stability, and productivity. The real problem is a basic equation: we cut revenue, kept spending, and pretended the math would work out.

It didn't.

Cutting taxes for the wealthy while continuing to fund wars, subsidize corporations, and maintain a bloated defense budget is a guaranteed way to create a structural deficit. And that deficit accrues interest. Compound interest. So while billionaires are buying sports teams and yachts, the rest of us are paying the bill—twice.

Once through underfunded schools, broken transit, and crumbling infrastructure.
Again through interest payments on the tax breaks they lobbied for.

This is why raising taxes on the wealthy isn't extreme—it's overdue. It's not just about funding new programs. It's about slowing the bleeding. Stabilizing the patient. Paying down the bill for a party we didn't get invited to.

Because until we do that, every promise from our government starts with a lie. Every infrastructure plan. Every public housing project. Every budget with good intentions and no path to fund it.

You can't build a better country on debt denial. And you can't keep pretending that billionaires are somehow doing their fair share.

They aren't. But you are. And you're the one being asked to sacrifice more.

It's time to flip that.

Tariffs Are Taxes; Subsidies Are Strategy

Let's be blunt: tariffs are just taxes in disguise. When the government slaps a tariff on an imported product, it's not the foreign company that pays—it's you. You pay more at checkout, more at the gas pump, more for any product that crosses a border. And unless that tariff is part of a real, long-term industrial strategy, it's not policy. It's posturing.

Raising prices on purpose isn't a solution—it's a stall tactic. A smoke screen that looks tough while doing very little to improve American life.

A smarter approach is to fund what we want to grow—not punish what we don't. In other words, subsidies beat tariffs. When used correctly, they shape the future.
Look at China. For years, the Chinese government has built out massive transportation infrastructure—railways, highways, and electric vehicle networks. When global oil prices spiked, they didn't just ride it out—they subsidized domestic travel and EV

infrastructure to keep people moving. That's not luck. That's planning.

Now compare that to the U.S., where we throw tariffs on solar panels, complain about gas prices, and wait for the market to fix itself.
If rising fuel costs are nudging Americans toward electric vehicles, then subsidize the shift. Don't just punish the alternative—invest in the solution. That means affordable EVs. That means charging stations in every neighborhood. That means making the cleaner choice the cheaper one.

We already subsidize fossil fuels to the tune of about $20 billion a year. That money could be redirected to energy storage, smart grids, and a clean-energy workforce. Not hypothetical. Not one day. Right now.

But energy isn't the only place where we get it wrong.
We spend billions propping up industrial agriculture while small farmers drown in debt. We've stockpiled over 1.5 billion pounds of processed cheese in cold storage—yes, actual government cheese caves—because of outdated dairy subsidies that reward overproduction no matter the demand.

We bail out airlines after they burn through profits on stock buybacks. We underfund public transit while giving tax breaks to car manufacturers who offshore their labor.

That's not economic policy. That's donor politics.

A true subsidy strategy should answer one clear question: What kind of economy are we trying to build?

If the goal is a resilient middle class, we should be investing in local food systems, green jobs, public infrastructure, and education—not padding the profit margins of legacy industries that treat the public like a backup wallet.

Stop calling tariffs strategy. Start calling smart subsidies what they are: long-term cost savings for the people who actually fund this country.

Tax Myths Debunked

Some tax myths are so baked into American culture that people treat them like gospel—repeating them year after year without ever questioning who benefits from the lie.

"I pay less taxes than the rich."

Maybe in raw dollars. But in percentage terms, many working- and middle-class Americans actually pay more. Once you add in payroll taxes, sales taxes, gas taxes, and all the local and state fees that quietly chip away at your income, the total burden often outweighs what ultra-wealthy individuals pay—especially when they park income offshore, claim paper losses, and structure their wealth to avoid traditional taxation altogether.

"Lower taxes mean more freedom."

That's only true if you can afford to replace what taxes were paying for. If your neighborhood has no functioning public school, no bus route, and no hospital within 20 miles, your "freedom" is really just isolation with a price tag. Freedom without access is a lie.

"Tax cuts grow the economy."

Sometimes, but it depends on where the cuts go. Tax cuts for lower- and middle-income people often get spent quickly—on groceries, rent, child care. That creates demand and stimulates growth. But tax cuts for the rich? They're far more likely to go into stock buybacks, luxury assets, or offshore holdings. That doesn't build anything. That just compounds wealth.

That's the heart of it: tax myths persist because they serve power. They create cover for policies that redistribute wealth upward while convincing the public they're the ones getting a break.

But you don't build a strong country on trickle-down economics. You build it on shared infrastructure, smart investment, and a tax code that reflects what we value—not just what we tolerate.

If we want a fairer system, we have to start by telling the truth about what the current one is actually doing.

You Already Paid for the Library

We love to romanticize those tiny roadside libraries—the "take a book, leave a book" boxes tucked into front yards and parks. They're sweet. They're neighborly. They make us feel like we still live in a world where people share what they have.

But here's the thing.
You already paid for a full library. With your taxes. Every year.

And it's not just a place for books. It's a place for job seekers, parents, seniors, students, immigrants, and anyone who needs Wi-Fi, shelter, a resume workshop, or just a quiet place to sit. Libraries offer after-school programs. Story time for toddlers. Cooling stations during heat waves. Voter registration. Access to printers and scanners. Even lunch.
But we treat them like outdated relics. Or worse, as budget line items to be slashed.

That's the irony. We celebrate the little free library box like it's proof of community—and forget that the actual community investment already exists. We just stopped defending it.

We shouldn't need charity to survive. We shouldn't rely on crowdsourcing and side hustles to patch holes in public infrastructure. And we definitely shouldn't be treating basic services as luxuries.

You don't need to donate. You already did.

The real question is whether your money is being used well—or being siphoned off before it ever gets to the places that matter.

Taxes aren't theft. They're your collective down payment on the world you said you wanted to live in.

The IRS Is Not the Enemy

The IRS isn't here to ruin your spring. It's here to fund your future. But for decades, it's been underfunded, over-politicized, and turned into a scapegoat—by the very people who benefit from keeping it weak.

Here's what most people don't know. If you make under $200,000 a year, you're about five times more likely to be audited than someone making over $5 million. That's not a glitch—it's the result of strategic defunding. The less money the IRS has, the fewer complex audits it can perform. And rich people's tax returns are the most complex of all.

So instead, the agency goes after easier cases—low- and middle-income filers, small business owners, gig workers. The ones without legal teams.

And it's not just about who gets audited. It's about how much money we never even collect. The IRS estimates that the annual "tax gap"—the difference between what's owed and what's paid—is around $160 billion, and most of that comes from high-income earners underreporting income or hiding it through loopholes.

But let's be honest. The wealthy don't do this alone.

They're enabled.
By the tax attorneys who specialize in shell companies.
By the CPAs who build entire businesses on aggressive avoidance.
By the wealth managers who set up offshore trusts and dodgy write-offs.
By the banks who help hide assets across borders.

And they do it knowing they're unlikely to face consequences.

That's what should make you angry.

Because while you're paying your share—and probably paying more than your share—there's an entire economy of financial professionals who exist solely to help the richest Americans skip out on theirs.

So no, don't hate the IRS. Hate the enablers. The ones who profit off a rigged system and then sell their services like it's just smart strategy.
Maybe it's time we stopped treating this as cleverness and started treating it like what it really is: fraud at scale.

If a nurse lies on their taxes, they risk penalties and back payments. But if a billionaire lies—through layers of accountants and legal shields—it's considered savvy. That double standard is rotting the core of what taxes are meant to be: shared contribution, not selective obedience.

So here's one proposal. If you're a licensed CPA or attorney caught knowingly helping a client evade taxes at scale— millions or tens of millions—you lose that license. And depending on the damage? Maybe you lose your freedom too.

Because if we're serious about funding a functioning society, then we need to hold accountable the people who are gutting its foundation from the inside.

This isn't about punishment for the sake of punishment. It's about trust. You can't ask working people to do their part while letting the wealthy rewrite the rules.

The IRS isn't the villain. It's the calculator. The problem is who gets to use the eraser.

Tariffs, Social Security, and the USPS: What Actually Works

People love to talk about tariffs—like taxing imported goods is some magic lever that fixes everything. But here's the truth: tariffs don't build strong economies. They create new costs at home, not just abroad. Companies pass those costs onto consumers. Prices rise. Trade partners retaliate. The cycle keeps feeding itself—until the people hurt most are the same working- and middle-class families politicians claim to protect.

We're seeing it play out right now in 2025. Tariffs on imports are driving up the cost of basic goods—while doing little to actually strengthen domestic industries. It's economic theater that punishes the people buying groceries and paying rent, not the corporations at the top.

If we want real, sustainable progress, there are better levers to pull.

Take Social Security. The richest Americans stop paying Social Security taxes once they hit the income cap—around $160,000 a year. That means someone making $10 million pays the same as someone making $160,000. Remove the cap, and you shore up the program for generations—without raising rates on the middle class.

And the USPS? Congress still requires it to pre-fund retiree benefits 70 years in advance—an impossible standard no private business meets. Reduce that to something realistic—30 or 35 years—and we stabilize one of the most trusted public services we have. We lower the cost of mail, protect rural delivery, and maybe stop pretending Amazon's two-day shipping is the gold standard society actually needs.

Kintsugi and the Broken Bowl

Every coach I ever played for—from middle school through college—said the same thing before we left an away game: "Leave the locker room better than we found it." It didn't matter if we won or lost. Didn't matter how tough the game was. You cleaned up, picked up after your team, and left that space better than it was when you arrived.
It stuck with me. Because it wasn't about towels on the floor. It was about respect—for the place, for the people who came next, and for the opportunity to be part of something bigger than yourself.

That's how we should think about government. About taxes. About democracy.

Not as something broken and disposable—but as a system that can be repaired, restored, and improved. A system worth leaving better than we found it.

There's a Japanese philosophy called Kintsugi—the art of repairing broken pottery with gold. The idea is that the break is part of the object's history. You don't hide the cracks. You honor them. You fill them with something stronger. The repaired object becomes more valuable not in spite of the damage, but because of it.
That's what we need to do now.

We don't need a new bowl. We need to repair the one we have—with honesty, transparency, and pressure. We need to stop pretending the system isn't cracked and start asking how we can make it stronger where it broke.
Our tax code has been shattered and patched in ways that benefit the powerful. Our public trust has been chipped away. But the answer isn't to walk away. The answer is to fill those

fractures with gold—by demanding accountability, rebuilding what works, and refusing to settle for a government that only serves the few.

A repaired democracy shouldn't hide its scars. It should show how it healed.

And that healing starts with us.

Why Voting Is a Financial Decision

We don't talk enough about voting as a money issue. But it is.

Want lower rent? Better healthcare? Safer neighborhoods? Then you need to vote. Because every budget is a reflection of priorities—and politicians decide what gets funded. If you don't show up, someone else's priorities win. And you'll feel it in your paycheck, your commute, your ER bill, your kid's classroom.

Voter suppression and political apathy aren't just tactics. They're economic weapons. Keeping working people away from the ballot box is the fastest way to protect wealth at the top.

And make no mistake—we've been here before. The first Gilded Age only broke when voters forced change through labor reforms, antitrust laws, and progressive taxation. We're back in that same cycle now, facing consolidated corporate power and a government too often captured by wealth. The only way out is the same as it was then: people showing up, demanding better, and refusing to let policy be written solely by the rich.

And apathy? That's the real jackpot for the powerful. In local elections across the country, turnout often falls below 30%. In some cities, it's under 20%. That's not democracy. That's a boardroom meeting with a ballot.

And when turnout is low, it doesn't mean nobody wins—it means lobbyists win. Developers win. Private equity wins. The people who don't need your school to work or your bus line to run or your water to be safe—those are the people who benefit when you stay home.

That's why the fight over voting access is really a fight over money. Who gets it. Who keeps it. Who sees a return on the taxes we all pay.

Remember, at an average salary, you'd need 10,000 years to reach a billion dollars. That's not grit—that's a system hoarding wealth for centuries while you're told to cut coupons and skip lattes. Your vote is the only tool you have to reclaim that kind of imbalance and redirect those fortunes back into schools, hospitals, and infrastructure that actually serve you.

So let's cut through the noise. Ignore the culture war bait. The outrage cycles. The carefully timed political drama. Because those aren't issues—they're distractions.

They want you angry about a book in a school library so you don't notice your public school can't afford a nurse. They want you fired up about flags so you don't see the housing bond that could actually lower your rent.

In the end, every vote comes down to one thing: will this candidate raise taxes on the rich to fund public goods? Or will they cut taxes and gut services?

That's the real ballot. Every time. Everything else is just noise. What shows up on your ballot might not look like a big moment. It might be a school funding line. A housing measure. A public safety bond. A local tax that funds bus routes, park maintenance, or after-school programs.

That's exactly why it matters.

Because what happens in your neighborhood isn't decided by Twitter. It's decided by turnout.

Billionaires spend millions convincing you your vote doesn't matter. And they're right—if you believe them.

But if you vote? If you organize? If you show up and bring five friends with you?

That's when the calculus changes. That's when your budget stops being dictated by someone else's donations and starts reflecting your life.

Voting isn't just a civic duty. It's economic self-defense.

Vote for Jobs That Still Exist

The next wave of economic disruption won't come from trade wars or budget cuts—it'll come from technology. Artificial intelligence is already reshaping how businesses operate. But whether it reshapes your job for the better—or replaces it entirely—depends on who's in charge when the shift hits.
Not all AI is bad. It can streamline repetitive tasks, speed up processes, even save lives. But left unchecked, it becomes a cost-cutting machine—replacing cashiers, designers, analysts, and content creators, all in the name of "efficiency."

That's not innovation. That's consolidation. That's profit growth at the expense of paychecks.
If you vote for candidates who treat AI like a magic trick instead of a labor issue, you're not voting for the future—you're voting for your own obsolescence. We need leaders who will tax AI-driven productivity gains, protect displaced workers, and require companies to invest in worker retraining before gutting jobs.

In the same way automation replaced factory jobs, generative AI is poised to hit the white-collar workforce—and fast. If your representatives don't understand that, or worse, don't care, then they're not on your side.

The question isn't whether AI will change work. It's whether it will erase the worker.

And here's the irony. If AI were actually designed for logic and efficiency—it would start at the top.
Feed a machine the salary data, stock buyback records, and golden parachute clauses of America's CEOs, and it wouldn't target the warehouse.
It would fire the C-suite.

But that's not how it works—because this isn't about logic. It's about leverage.
Automation, in the wrong hands, becomes a tool to protect power and slash labor from the bottom up.

That's why this is a voting issue. Because without policy guardrails, the future won't be efficient—it'll just be empty.

Bad Policy Is a Price Tag

We talk a lot about taxes, but we rarely talk about the hidden taxes—the ones you feel at the grocery store, at the car dealership, at the pharmacy. That's what tariffs do.

In 2025, tariffs on imported goods triggered price spikes and product shortages across the country. It wasn't foreign companies footing the bill—it was you. You paid more for the same things. You stood in longer lines. You got hit twice: once at checkout, and again when the job market cooled.

That's the real impact of bad economic policy. It doesn't show up on your pay stub—it shows up in your pantry, your rent, and your savings account.

And when imports drop, it's not just about supply chains. It's about demand. When companies stop ordering goods, it often means they're anticipating a slowdown. Less spending. Fewer jobs. A recession.

Don't wait for the headlines to tell you it's a crisis. If you've already felt the price hikes, if you've noticed delays and layoffs creeping in—this is your early warning. Your vote is your counterpunch.

Elections aren't just about culture wars or party loyalty. They're about what kind of economy we build—and who pays the price when it falters.

Where the Money Goes (Final Call to Action)

You don't fix a broken democracy by walking away. You fix it by showing up—with votes, with questions, with pressure. You hold power by holding receipts.

Every tax you pay is money already spent. The only question is who decided where it went. Every ballot you cast is a budget decision—your say in whether that money goes to billion-dollar jets or kindergarten teachers, stock buybacks or school lunches.

A government that invests in its people makes life cheaper for everyone. Safer streets, healthier families, better jobs—all of it flows downstream from smart spending. Taxes aren't theft. They're shared leverage.

If the system feels cracked, it's because it is. But cracks aren't the end. They're the beginning of repair. And just like in Kintsugi, the gold goes in the gaps. That's where the strength returns. That's where we begin again.

We've already said in law that fortunes up to roughly $10 million can move tax-free. Everything beyond that—hundreds of millions, billions of dollars—should finally be part of rebuilding the country that made those fortunes possible.

So vote like your paycheck depends on it. Budget like your community depends on it. Because this country isn't just ours to criticize—it's ours to reallocate.

Chapter 12: Investing for the Long Game

L et me get this out of the way up front:
This is not financial advice.

I'm not a financial advisor. I don't have a license, and I'm not going to tell you what to buy. I'm just someone who's watched the market across multiple economic storms—from the dot-com crash to the Great Recession, through COVID, and now into whatever this limbo is where inflation rises, wages stall, and the Fed feels like a coin toss.

Along the way, I earned a business degree and an MBA from one of the top programs in the world. I spent years working in economics, competitive strategy, and market intelligence—watching how money moves through systems, companies, and lives.

And here's the most important thing I've learned:

The game isn't about winning.
The game is about staying in long enough for the system to work.
It's the old fable all over again. The tortoise doesn't win because it's faster—it wins because it stays in the race. That's investing.

And yes—there is a system. One that was built, shaped, and maintained by government policy. Retirement accounts like 401(k)s, tax-deferred growth, capital gains rates—none of that happens in a vacuum. The tools are available because public policy made them available.

But they only help if you use them.
They only exist if we fight to protect them.

This chapter isn't about what to buy.
It's about how to think—especially when everyone else is thinking short-term.

Because the real trick isn't outsmarting the market.
It's not getting scared out of it.

We've Been Here Before.

You might be thinking… if the system's rigged, why stay in it at all?

Fair question.

But here's the truth: rigged doesn't mean broken for everyone. It means broken for most—but wildly effective for the few who already know how to stay in long enough for it to work in their favor. The tools exist because policy made them exist. And if you understand how to use them—if you stay in the game instead of opting out—you don't have to be rich to benefit. You just have to be consistent.

This isn't new.

In the late 1800s, America entered what we now call the Gilded Age. Wealth was hoarded at the top, corporations operated without oversight, and workers barely scraped by while tycoons built empires. Sound familiar?

Today, we're seeing the same patterns return. Power is consolidating. Lobbyists are writing the rules. Billionaires are paying tax rates lower than schoolteachers. The old playbook is still in play: weaken oversight, reward capital over labor, and convince the public that government is the enemy.

But not every country bought that story.

Places like Germany, Canada, and the U.K. strengthened government instead of shrinking it. They taxed wealth. They invested in public goods. They built systems that helped regular people stay afloat—without gambling on the stock market or winning the lottery.

We made a different choice.
But that doesn't mean we're stuck with it forever.

The first Gilded Age ended with a reckoning: trust-busting, labor protections, income taxes. Ordinary people demanded more from the system they were funding. And they got it— because they showed up.

If this really is a second Gilded Age, then it's not a reason to check out. It's a reason to double down. To learn the rules. To stay in the game. To push for a system that doesn't just work for the wealthy—it works for everyone.

You don't fight corruption by giving up.
You fight it by showing up with knowledge, consistency, and leverage.
And investing—even boring, quiet investing—is part of that leverage.

The Real Meaning of Investing

At its core, investing is just delayed spending.

You're choosing not to use the money today—so your future self has choices tomorrow. Not yachts. Not private jets. Just freedom. Stability. Time. Room to breathe.

But that's not how most people talk about investing.

They talk about it like a jackpot. Like a test of cleverness. A game where the right tip or the right trade might launch them into a different life.

It's sold like hope. Branded like ambition.
But it's built on math.

Here's the math: unless you're already rich—or breaking the law—you're not going to get wealthy overnight. You're not going to outguess the pros. You're not going to find the secret stock that triples before lunch. And you're not going to beat the system by skipping the hard part.

There is no secret.
There is no hack.
There's just consistency.

Investing isn't a test—it's a timeline.
Your job is to stay on the path long enough for the system to do its job.

That's the boring truth wealthy people already know. They don't gamble. They build. Slowly. Quietly. Safely. Over time, that boring approach becomes powerful.

Because when you need less to live, and you have even a modest investment growing quietly in the background… you start to win.

Not by outsmarting the market—but by outlasting the chaos.

When Interest Rates Are on Your Side

Interest rates get a bad rap—and for good reason. They make mortgages more expensive. Credit card debt heavier. Student loans harder to pay down.

But they aren't always the enemy.

Sometimes, they're a quiet ally… if you know how to use them. When rates rise, borrowing costs more—but saving earns more. Suddenly, your money sitting in a high-yield savings account or a Treasury-backed fund is working harder for you. You're not just preserving cash—you're collecting interest. Safely. Quietly. With no extra effort.
But here's the catch: high rates don't last.

Historically, when the Federal Reserve raises interest rates, it eventually lowers them again to avoid a recession. That means the current moment—where 4% to 5% yields on safe accounts exist—isn't permanent. It's a season.

So if you've built your emergency fund, and you're sweeping leftovers from your active spending budget at the end of each pay cycle—don't let them sit idle. Put those dollars somewhere they can do something. Somewhere they can grow.

This isn't about chasing returns. It's about being ready. Ready for rates to drop. Ready for costs to rise. Ready for your future.

The system isn't always fair. But sometimes, it is functional. And the people who benefit most are the ones who understand how to shift with it.

Your leftover money is your most flexible tool… but the long game isn't just about you. It's also about what your money keeps doing for the people and causes you care about.

When the Story Ends, the Math Shouldn't Get Messy

Most of us plan for everything… retirement, housing, emergencies… but we rarely plan for the one guarantee in life— that it ends. It's uncomfortable to think about, but preparing for it isn't morbid—it's generous. A will isn't about death… it's about kindness. It's about making life easier for the people— and communities—you leave behind.

And here's something most people don't talk about: planning ahead also removes stress for the ones you love. I've heard so many stories of families left scrambling—trying to find accounts, passwords, even funeral instructions—while they're still in shock. My mom made sure I'd never go through that. When I came home from my freshman year of college, she took me to set up my first will. She wanted to make sure I understood what peace feels like when things are handled. Over two decades later, I still don't have to be anxious about when she passes. I'll just be grieving… and celebrating her life.

Whether you have family, a partner, or a favorite nonprofit, clarity matters. Who gets your savings? Your car? The royalties from your creative work? If you don't decide, the state will… and the state won't care what mattered most to you.

When you take control of those decisions, you're not just protecting assets—you're protecting your values. You're deciding what kind of mark your life leaves behind.

You don't need a lawyer to start. Most states have simple will templates. Even my local San Diego Humane Society offers estate planning guides for supporters—it's not about wealth… it's about intention. The same idea exists in communities everywhere.

Write it down. Sign it. Store it safely. Tell one trusted person where it is. Your final act of financial literacy is making sure your life's work—and the things you cared about—keep making a difference.

Protecting your investments also means protecting your community… because the money you leave behind can still build, heal, and feed the world you believed in. That's the real long game—making sure your story keeps doing good even after you stop writing it.

Legacy planning reminds us that money isn't the goal—it's the tool. And once you've done the work to protect what you've built, you can get back to the next question that matters… how to make it grow while you're still here.

Because the long game isn't just about years in the market… it's about the kind of life you build — and the peace you leave behind.

The Lie of "10% Returns"

You've probably heard the stat that the stock market returns 10% annually on average.

And it's true… mathematically. From 1928 to 2024, the S&P 500 has averaged just over 10% per year. But averages are sneaky. They hide the rollercoaster underneath.

In nearly a century of data, the market has landed within 2% of that average—between 8% and 12%—only six times.

Six. Out of almost 100 years.

That means most years are not normal. Some are brutal. Others are euphoric. One year might be down 35%. The next might be up 28%. And when you zoom out far enough, the math smooths it all into something that sounds predictable.

But the ride isn't smooth. It's volatile. You only benefit from the average if you stay in the whole time.

That's why timing the market almost never works. Because the second you panic and pull out after a dip, the math stops working in your favor. You don't get the bounce back. You don't get the recovery. You get the regret.

So yes, the 10% stat is technically real. But it's not a promise. It's a probability—and only for the people who stayed in long enough to see it work.

What Investing Actually Feels Like

Real investing doesn't feel like success. It feels like waiting.

It feels like putting money into a fund when the headlines say the world is ending.
It feels like watching a friend double their money on crypto while you gain 3% in your index fund.
It feels like being bored… and trusting that boredom is the point.

If you're doing it right, investing feels uneventful. That's how you know it's not gambling. It's not supposed to spike your adrenaline. It's supposed to run in the background while you build your life.

The people who get excited are usually the ones taking on more risk than they can afford to lose. When that risk collapses, they're the ones who can't stay in. They have to cash out. They need the money back.

But if your expenses are under control, your income is steady, and your lifestyle doesn't require every dollar you make… you can stay in. You can ride out the dips.

That's the real win: not needing your investments right away. Boredom isn't a problem.
It's a privilege.

The Easy Button: Your 401(k)

If your job offers a 401(k), that's your starting line. And if they offer a match? That's not a perk—it's a raise. That's free money.

Most employer-sponsored retirement plans include something called a target-date fund. You pick the year you plan to retire—say, 2060—and the fund does the rest. It starts with more aggressive investments like stocks, then gradually shifts toward safer ones like bonds as your retirement date gets closer.

You don't have to micromanage it. You don't have to know what to buy. You don't have to check the news every week or move things around when the market gets weird.

You just have to start.

Set it. Forget it. Let it grow.

If you think back to Chapter 3, we talked about sweeping a few dollars out of every paycheck automatically—treating savings like rent you pay to your future self.

Investing works the same way. The best investors don't rely on willpower or perfectly timed decisions. They rely on automation.

The day your paycheck lands, that money can already be moving—to your 401(k), your Roth IRA, or an index fund—without you having to think about it.

Here's how it adds up:

- $42 per paycheck = $3 a day, over $1,000 a year.
- $100 per paycheck = $2,600 a year.
- That's before market growth, dividends, or compound returns kick in.

You don't have to pick the perfect number. You just have to pick a number—something you won't miss day-to-day—and let it move automatically. If your budget shifts, you can adjust.

This is how real wealth gets built—not with windfalls or risky bets, but with consistent, invisible moves that quietly accumulate in the background.

The people who get ahead don't treat investing as "extra." They treat it as a required cost of living, just like rent or insurance. It's a bill you pay to your future self… and it's one bill you'll never regret paying.

That's the quiet power of automation. It pulls investing out of the emotional zone and into the routine zone. You won't notice it right away—but over time, it becomes the foundation of your financial freedom.

This is where boring starts to look brilliant.

The Roth Advantage: Tax Me Now, Thank Me Later

There's something liberating about knowing the money you've invested is already yours. No future tax bill. No surprise clawback. No wondering what the rates will be when you retire.

That's the quiet beauty of the Roth 401(k) and Roth IRA. You pay taxes on the money today—when your income (and therefore your tax rate) might be lower—and in exchange, you get tax-free growth forever. That's right: forever.

You can't always predict future policy. But betting that tax rates won't rise over the next few decades? That's not a financial strategy—it's a fantasy. Roths aren't just a savings tool—they're a hedge against fiscal policy uncertainty.

If you're eligible, open one. Fund it as early in the year as you can. If you've already maxed out your 401(k)—traditional or Roth—put money toward a Roth IRA next. And remember— Roths don't exist by accident. They're the result of policy choices. Which means if we don't demand policies that protect them, we risk losing the very tools that make long-term freedom possible.

Stocks vs. Index Funds: The Coin Flip Analogy

This is how I explain stocks vs. index funds to friends.

Let's say you have $20.

Option A: Bet it all on one coin flip.
Heads, you double it. Tails, you lose everything.

Option B: Split it into five bets—$4 each—and flip five separate coins.
Now if three of them land heads, you still come out ahead.

That's the difference.

With a single stock, you're betting on one company to pull through. If it soars, great. But if it crashes, you're done. There's no cushion.
An index fund spreads that bet across hundreds of companies. Some will fail. Some will rise. And over time, the winners usually outweigh the losers.

You're not trying to find the next Apple. You're trying to own enough of the economy that you benefit no matter which company becomes the next Apple.

It's not about luck. It's about math. That's what diversification really is.

Index funds aren't loud. They don't spike. But they work—quietly, reliably, and long-term.

What I Learned in My MBA Program

At UCLA, we didn't sit around debating Reddit threads or guessing which stock might spike next. We studied the systems —the same ones the wealthy already use.

And let's be honest: some of them are playing a different game entirely.

- Members of Congress trade stocks in companies they regulate.
- Insiders buy shares right before earnings announcements.
- Accredited investors get into private equity rounds before the public even knows the company exists.
- The ultra-wealthy avoid taxes by borrowing against assets instead of selling them—paying less in taxes than most teachers or nurses.

This isn't conspiracy. It's structure.

ProPublica found that the richest Americans paid an effective tax rate of just 3.4% over several years—because the system lets them. Meanwhile, you're taxed every time your paycheck hits the bank.

That's why regular people can't afford to gamble. That's why we need insulation—not instinct.

What I saw again and again was this: the rich don't play to win big. They play not to lose.

They hedge.
They buy index funds.
They reinvest dividends.
They build systems that grow quietly, safely, and tax-efficiently over time.

They're not trying to get rich. They're trying to stay rich.

That was the biggest lesson I took from business school. Wealth isn't about taking big swings. It's about building boring habits... and refusing to get knocked out of the game.

Hope Costs More Than You Think

Let's talk about the lottery.

If you spend $10 a week on tickets for 20 years, that's over $10,000. If you had invested that same amount with steady returns, you'd likely have more than triple that today.

Lotteries are often called a "tax on the poor," but that's not quite right. They're a tax on desperation. They sell the illusion of escape to people who feel like they don't have another option.

And crypto? It's the same hustle—just shinier. New language, new platforms, same outcome.

Let me say this as clearly as I can:

Crypto is not a currency.
It's not backed by revenue, earnings, or real-world use.
It's not regulated like stocks, protected like banks, or governed like bonds.
It's speculative by design.

If you want to dabble? Fine. But treat it like poker, not a plan. Don't call it investing. Don't build your retirement on a meme. And don't let influencers sell you "freedom" while they cash out at your expense.

Hope is not a strategy.
And in the financial world, hope is expensive.

That's why people with wealth avoid hype. They don't chase moonshots—they build baselines. They don't buy dreams. They build dividends.

Because when you stop hoping for a miracle...
You start planning for real freedom.

So What Actually Works?

Here's the cheat sheet no one's selling you—because you can't wrap it in a course or slap it on TikTok.

- Index funds win long-term. Not always flashy, but historically consistent.
- Roth IRAs grow tax-free. That flexibility matters more than people realize.
- 401(k) matches are a 100% return. If your employer offers one, take it. Every time.
- Start early. Time beats amount. Every. Single. Time.
- Avoid high-fee advisors. They don't have to beat the market to get rich—because they're skimming yours.
- You can't time the market. You'll miss the dip... and the recovery.
- Set it. Forget it. Stay the course. That's the real magic.

Here's the crazy part:

If you invest from age 25 to 35—and then stop—you'll often end up with more than someone who starts at 35 and invests the same amount every year until retirement.

Why?
Because compound growth is brutal, beautiful math—and it rewards the early.
It's not fair. But it's real.

So the best plan isn't perfect.
It's consistent. And it starts now—with whatever you've got.

Why Millionaires Drive Hondas

Most millionaires aren't rolling up in Ferraris. They're driving Hondas, Toyotas, maybe a used Lexus if they splurged. It's not because they can't afford more—it's because they don't need to.

They're not spending money to look rich.
They're using money to stay rich.

The real flex isn't leasing a car that eats half your paycheck. It's having enough cash to walk away from a bad boss... or a bad system... and still be okay.

Wealth doesn't shout.
It doesn't flash.
It doesn't need to be seen.

It sits in accounts that grow while you sleep. It buys back your time. It waits patiently for the moments that matter—whether it's a family emergency, a career pivot, or a chance to help someone else.

The people who win this game aren't the ones with the biggest bets.
They're the ones who stayed in the longest.

What If You Don't Invest?

This is the part that often gets overlooked.

Even with growing efforts to encourage retirement savings— like California's CalSavers program, which mandates employers to offer retirement plans—many people still aren't investing.

If you don't invest, you're not just missing out. You're falling behind.

Inflation erodes your savings.

Rising rents outpace wage growth.
Healthcare costs continue to climb.
The market keeps moving… without you.

You might find yourself with fewer options and more financial stress—not because you were reckless, but because you didn't have the tools or knowledge to navigate the system effectively.

The system doesn't necessarily reward brilliance.
It rewards consistency.

It doesn't punish risk-takers.
It often penalizes the cautious and the uninformed.

But once you recognize this, you can take steps to change your financial trajectory.

You don't need to master the market.
You just need to participate in it.

Retirement Isn't a Finish Line

It's tempting to think of retirement as the grand finale — the day you clock out for good and finally "stop worrying." But retirement isn't a finish line. It's just another phase where your daily burn rate still matters.

The same math applies:

- Your passive costs don't disappear.
- Your active choices still shape your freedom.
- Your money either stretches or shrinks based on how much control you keep.

Even in retirement, clarity is power. The people who feel trapped later in life aren't the ones who failed to chase the right hot stock. They're the ones who carried too much debt, too many fixed costs, and too little flexibility.

If you want dignity in retirement, don't treat it as a separate universe. Treat it as a continuation of the same principles you've been applying all along.

This Isn't About Getting Rich. It's About Getting Free.

Investing isn't supposed to feel exciting. It's not supposed to feel like a win.
It's supposed to feel stable. Quiet. Even boring.

Because that's what freedom feels like.

It's not the thrill of a crypto spike or the adrenaline of timing the market just right.
It's being able to say yes to something meaningful… without checking your balance first.
It's being able to leave a toxic job… and know you'll be okay.
It's walking into the next chapter of your life with options, not panic.

That's what investing buys you:
Not a yacht. Not a private jet.
Just room to breathe. Room to move. Room to build.

Every dollar you invest isn't just growing—it's casting a vote for your future.
Not someone else's.

When that future shows up—unexpectedly, beautifully, or urgently—you'll be able to say yes… because you stayed the course.

Chapter 13: Healthcare

Y ou can do everything right—eat well, exercise, work full-time, buy insurance—and still go bankrupt if you get sick.

In most countries, getting healthy is a path back to life.
In the United States, it's a path into debt.

We don't have a healthcare system.
We have a billing system with some nurses attached.

And if the goal of this country is truly "life, liberty, and the pursuit of happiness," then how are we letting for-profit corporations decide who gets to live—just to defend their quarterly earnings?

The truth is, health isn't just a personal matter. It's financial. It's systemic. It shapes our jobs, our housing, our ability to plan a future. It quietly dominates our spending—even when we think we're healthy.

This chapter isn't about insurance jargon. It's about the system you're already trapped inside, the one that's costing you money whether you use it or not... and what smarter spending could look like if we had the courage to do things differently.

My Story: Ulcerative Colitis and Corporate Captivity

I was diagnosed with Ulcerative Colitis at 20. I had just helped win a Division I national championship in lacrosse and was in the best shape of my life. Still, despite all that, the insurance company's recommendation was to remove my intestines and live with a colostomy bag. Not because it was the best medical option—but because it was cheaper than covering the ongoing prescription care I needed.

That's not just ridiculous. It's terrifying.

Before the Affordable Care Act passed, I lived with constant, invisible pressure:
Don't lose your job. Don't lose your insurance.

It shaped everything. I didn't stay in corporate strategy because it lit my soul on fire—I stayed because I couldn't afford to lose coverage. I didn't use my fifth year of eligibility, even though I could have. I didn't want my mom paying another $50,000 for college just so I could keep playing lacrosse.

I didn't start a business because "follow your passion" doesn't mean much when your immune system is on a hair trigger and every gap in care could send you to the ER.

This didn't just impact how I spent money—it shaped my entire adult life.
And I'm one of the lucky ones.

The Real Players Behind Rising Costs

Let's break down the system:

- **Insurance companies** aim to minimize payouts and maximize profit. Denials aren't mistakes—they're the model. The less they pay, the more they make.
- **Hospitals** have to turn beds quickly, keep labor costs low, and maximize procedural billing to stay financially afloat.
- **Doctors** often carry six figures in student debt and work grueling hours to meet quotas set by hospital administrators—quotas that prioritize billable codes over patient outcomes.
- **Travel nurses** are among the few with negotiating power, thanks to their flexibility and high demand—but their higher pay is often used as a scapegoat to mask broader staffing mismanagement.
- **Administrative overhead** is a hidden tax on everyone. Studies published in JAMA and by the Peterson-KFF Health System Tracker show that administrative expenses account for 15% to 25% of U.S. healthcare spending—nearly double the share seen in other developed nations.
- **Pharmaceutical companies** profit from monopoly rights, not just innovation. Many breakthrough drugs begin in taxpayer-funded university labs, then get patented and sold back at prices that far exceed their development costs. Most companies rely on acquisitions to fill weak pipelines, not true discovery. Once a drug clears about $2 billion in sales, the rest is pure profit—yet patents can stretch on for decades, locking patients into sky-high prices.

Stack all of that together and who's holding the bag?

You are. With rising premiums, missed paychecks, and the kind of stress that doesn't just keep you up at night—it wears down your body over time.

The average premium for single coverage is over $8,400 per year. That doesn't include your deductible, co-pays, or the surprise bill for the out-of-network anesthesiologist you didn't even know was assigned to you.

And somehow, we've accepted this.

The System Isn't Confusing. It's Designed This Way.

You're not crazy for struggling to pick a plan. You're in a maze —one designed by people who make money every time you take a wrong turn.

Employers push high-deductible HSA plans—not because they help you—but because they're cheaper for the company. FSAs (Flexible Spending Accounts) let you set aside pre-tax money for healthcare costs, but the catch is use-it-or-lose-it. HSAs (Health Savings Accounts) are tied to high-deductible insurance and pitched as tax-advantaged "savings vehicles," but most people never reach the investing stage because the deductible eats them alive first.

The FSA vs. HSA Trap

Here's where I land: the so-called "high deductible + HSA" plan is often a trap. Yes, your employer might toss in a few hundred bucks for free, but the tradeoff is a deductible so high you'll be on the hook for thousands before insurance even kicks in. That's not savings. That's gambling with your health.

A smarter play? Pick the medium-tier insurance plan. It balances your monthly premium with a manageable deductible so one bad month doesn't sink your budget. Then, fund an FSA only to the level of your actual needs—your prescriptions, co-pays, glasses, therapy sessions. It lowers your taxable income, and you don't risk getting crushed by surprise bills.

The HSA might look shiny, but most people never get past the deductible to enjoy the "investment account" part. The FSA, capped though it is, at least matches reality: use what you need, when you need it.

This isn't a perfect solution—it's survival mode until we build something better.

Prescription Chaos

If picking a plan feels like a trap, just wait until you try to fill a prescription.

Prescription pricing is a masterclass in chaos. No one—not even your pharmacist—can tell you the real price until the computer spits it out. And those "prior authorizations" that make you wait for care? They're not about safety. They're about stalling until you give up or find a way to pay out of pocket.

We've normalized a system where even having insurance still leaves you afraid to get sick. And that fear doesn't live in the abstract—it lives in your calendar, your bank account, and your bloodstream.

There's a Smarter Way to Pay

Let's stop pretending this isn't already a tax.

Right now, someone earning $40,000 a year is likely paying between 15% and 20% of their income on healthcare—once you combine premiums, deductibles, co-pays, prescriptions, and the wages lost from missed work or skipping shifts due to illness.

So let's just make it honest. And make it work.

Every developed nation with universal healthcare already does some version of what I'm proposing.

They pay through taxes—roughly 10% to 20% of income—but in return, no one fears an ambulance bill or loses a house over a diagnosis. The math is honest, the trade-off clear: one predictable cost instead of endless uncertainty.

In the United States, we already pay about that much... just in chaotic, fragmented ways.
The average individual premium alone is over $8,400 per year, while a family plan now tops $23,000—before deductibles, co-pays, and unpaid time off. The difference is, other countries call it healthcare. We call it stress.

So if we're already spending the equivalent of a universal system, why not design one that actually works?

The 20% Healthcare Tax

Here's what that would look like:

- Flat 20% tax on income, earmarked exclusively for healthcare
- No premiums
- No deductibles
- No co-pays
- No networks
- No job-lock

And this isn't a new cost. You're already paying:

- 1.45% Medicare payroll tax (plus your employer matches it)
- Federal taxes that fund Medicaid, hospital bailouts, and uncompensated care
- Thousands in premiums
- Thousands more out-of-pocket
- The hidden bill of avoiding care until it's too late

This doesn't add another layer. It simplifies the ones already suffocating you.

You pay once. You get care. No gimmicks. No gatekeeping. Just healthcare that shows up when you need it—without bankrupting your future.

What You Pay Now vs. What You'd Pay With Universal Care

Current System	20% Healthcare Tax Plan
$8,400+ average annual premium	Replaced with a predictable 20% contribution
Deductibles up to $3,000	No deductibles
Co-pays, coinsurance, "cost sharing"	No surprise fees
Surprise bills from "out-of-network" providers	Go anywhere. Get treated. Period.
Fear of job loss = loss of coverage	Coverage is tied to you, not your job
Multiple hidden taxes for public coverage	One transparent, direct contribution

You're not paying less now. You're just paying in confusing, chaotic ways—and still getting burned.

Break the Patent Monopoly

I'm all for patents. They protect ideas, reward innovation, and give creators a chance to profit from their work. But in healthcare, patents don't just create profit—they create death. A life-saving drug locked up for decades is not innovation. It's ransom.

If a drug has been on the market for five years or has earned $2 billion in sales—whichever comes first—the patent should end.

At that point, the company has recouped its costs and made plenty of money. From then on, competitors should be free to produce it so patients can afford to live.

Patents should encourage discovery, not hold life hostage.

Fix the Pipeline, Fix the Price

The crisis in healthcare isn't just what we pay—it's how we train the people we rely on.

Most doctors don't enter medicine for the paycheck. They enter it to help. But the system they step into is a debt trap disguised as a calling.

We load future providers with six-figure loans. We weed them out with academic hazing—classes like Organic Chemistry that have more to do with gatekeeping than patient care. We stretch training over a decade, demand perfection, and then act surprised when we don't have enough primary care doctors, nurses, or mental health professionals.

And then we wonder why people burn out. Why they quit. Why they never enter the field in the first place.

This isn't about lowering standards. It's about raising access. It's about designing a pipeline where every step is a viable stopping point—where people can enter, exit, and return without financial ruin.

Want to fix the healthcare system? Start with the people it needs to run. And stop breaking them before they even begin.

A Tiered, Flexible Medical Pipeline

Imagine a system where every step on the path leads to a viable job.
People can stop where it makes sense. They can come back when they're ready. Here's what that could look like:

Time	Credential	Role
2 Years	Medical Associate Cert	Tech / Assistant
4 Years	Clinical Bachelor's	Registered Nurse
5 Years	Advanced Clinical Degree	Physician Assistant
6–7 Years	Master's in Diagnostic Care	Nurse Practitioner
8+ Years	Doctor of Medicine	Physician

This kind of pipeline doesn't just lower costs. It speeds up time-to-impact.

Instead of forcing everyone through an eight-year gauntlet just to be useful, we create multiple exit points where people can contribute, earn a living, and return for more when ready. That means more techs, more nurses, more assistants—sooner.

It's not about flooding the field. It's about building a system that actually keeps up with demand.

Rural Care Through Rotation

Healthcare deserts are real.

Over 136 rural hospitals have closed since 2010.
More than 700 more are at risk.
Eighty percent of U.S. counties lack adequate access to primary care, trauma care, or pharmacies.

Over 60 percent of designated primary care shortage areas are rural.

This isn't just a healthcare problem—it's a geography problem. But it's also a national opportunity.

What if every newly trained provider—doctors, nurses, nurse practitioners, physician assistants—spent one to two years rotating through rural or underserved areas?

Housing support would be included.
Full salary. Mentorship.
Not punishment—service. A structured career stage. A deeper kind of education.

This wouldn't just help patients—it would help the providers. Because when you spend time in places you might never have chosen on your own, you build empathy. You build perspective. You build connection to a part of the country you might have never otherwise known.

Some providers will move on.
But some will stay—because they'll fall in love with the work, the pace, the people.
We saw it during COVID. People left cities. Some never came back.

This kind of rotation builds a national pipeline—not just of workers, but of understanding.
It brings new energy to towns that have been overlooked for decades. It brings diversity to places that don't often see it. It makes healthcare a vehicle for rebuilding the backbone of this country—not just its cities, but its communities.

It's not just care. It's presence. It's investment.
And it's long overdue.

What About Mental Health?

We can't talk about healthcare deserts without mentioning the quietest, deadliest one of all—mental health access.

In huge swaths of the country, there isn't a single licensed therapist within 50 miles. In urban areas, the waitlists are weeks long—or worse, it's out-of-pocket only, and insurance won't even touch it.

That's not just an inconvenience. It's a crisis.
Mental healthcare isn't a luxury. It's basic maintenance for the brain. And when you skip maintenance long enough, things break—relationships, jobs, sleep, physical health, all of it. The collapse is quiet at first. Then it's loud.

And it's happening everywhere.

In a universal care system, mental health wouldn't be carved out like it's optional. It would be core care—funded, covered, and protected, just like physical health. No more treating the brain like an add-on. No more pretending it's not part of the body.

No one should have to go broke just to feel okay. And no one should have to choose between groceries and grief counseling.

A healthcare system that leaves out mental health isn't really healthcare at all.

The Life & Disability Insurance Pitch

Healthcare isn't the only way medical risk drains your wallet. At some point, you'll get pitched life insurance or disability insurance — usually at work or from a financial rep who swears it's essential.

Here's the reality:

- Life insurance is only necessary if someone else depends on your income. And if you do need it, stick with term life. It's cheap, straightforward, and expires when your kids are grown or your mortgage is gone. The flashy versions — whole life, universal life, cash value — are mostly sales tactics. They masquerade as investments but mainly pad the agent's commission.
- Disability insurance is more complicated. If your job is physical, or your income is the sole support for a family, it can be worth it. But read every clause. Many policies are full of carve-outs that make them useless when you actually need them.

The test is simple: insurance should protect you from ruin, not inconvenience. Most of the time, these products are sold as fear in a contract. If you don't have dependents, skip the life insurance. If your household could survive a few months without your paycheck, skip the disability policy.

The Real Cost of Waiting

Every day we delay reform, people delay care.

They skip checkups. They ration insulin. They wait until the pain is unbearable—not because they're irresponsible, but because they're scared of the bill.

That's not a medical decision. It's a financial one.
Every time someone waits too long, the cost rises.
A cavity becomes a root canal.
A panic attack becomes an ER visit.
A sore knee becomes a permanent limp.
A treatable illness becomes a long-term disability.

This isn't just failing people. It's setting money on fire.

Because when you delay care, you pay twice—once through suffering, and again through more expensive treatment later. Preventive care is cheaper. Early care is more effective. But we've built a system that rewards neither.

Similarly, every time someone goes without care because of cost, the rest of the economy feels it. Missed work. Lost productivity. Early death. Burnout. Caregiver strain.

We don't save money by skimping on care.
We waste it.

A System That Spends Smarter

Right now, Americans spend more on healthcare than any other developed country—and get worse results.

We pay more than $8,000 a year in premiums.
We carry deductibles over $2,000.
We get hit with surprise bills.
We lose wages when we skip work to recover.
And when it's all too much? We declare bankruptcy.
Over 60 percent of personal bankruptcies in the U.S. involve medical debt. Not because people didn't plan—but because the system didn't care.

This chapter isn't asking you to spend more. It's asking you to stop spending stupid.

A 20 percent healthcare tax sounds big—until you realize you're already paying more than that in scattered, stressful, invisible ways. You just don't call it a tax. You call it your premium. Your copay. Your dread.

The goal here isn't more healthcare spending. It's better healthcare spending.
One payment. One system. One standard.

Financial freedom isn't just about income. It's about insulation —from chaos, collapse, and systems that punish you for getting sick.

We don't need to fund healthcare better. We need to stop funding it wrong.

Chapter 14: The Cost of Children and Pets

Who wants advice on parenting from someone without kids? Maybe you do. Maybe you don't. Either way, we all live in an economy shaped by the cost of raising children—even if we never have them ourselves.

Right now, raising kids isn't just a personal decision. It's an economic outlier.

We've reached a place where starting a family feels like a luxury good. Not biologically—economically. The cost of housing alone has made parenthood feel out of reach for many. Add in childcare, insurance, diapers, formula, rent inflation—and the dream of a family starts looking more like a financial crisis in slow motion.

Yet every day, people have kids. Some planned it. Some didn't. Some thought they were ready and realized they weren't. And some… just adjusted, because life doesn't always ask permission.

Whether your child arrives on schedule or as a total surprise, the financial reality is the same: love is one of the most expensive things you can ever spend time on. That doesn't make it a mistake. But it does mean you need to plan—even if the planning comes after the baby.

Because kids don't care whether you were "ready." They care whether there's enough.

Pets: The "Starter Family" That Costs More Than You Think

Before we even talk about raising kids, let's talk about the warm-up act: pets. For many of us, adopting a dog or cat feels like a simple, low-stakes way to start building a family. You spend a couple hundred dollars on adoption fees, pick up some food and a leash, and you're set... or so you think.

But pets have a way of turning into long-term, high-cost commitments—much closer to raising children than people like to admit. Over a dog's 12- to 15-year life, expenses like food, vet visits, flea medication, vaccinations, teeth cleanings, and the inevitable late-night emergency clinic runs can easily add up to $15,000–$30,000. Cats may be cheaper, but not by much once you factor in litter, scratching posts, and health issues later in life.

Then there are the hidden lifestyle costs:

- **Housing:** Many rentals add monthly "pet rent." I pay $75 per cat right now—$150 every month before a single can of food hits the bowl. That's $1,800 a year just for permission to have them in the apartment—and once you factor in food, litter, and routine vet care, the yearly cost easily climbs to $3,000 to $4,000.
- **Travel:** Boarding or pet-sitting adds up quickly. Bringing pets along means bigger vehicles, pet-friendly hotels, or avoiding flights altogether.
- **Emotional Spending:** When your veterinarian tells you your dog needs a $3,000 surgery, you're not weighing ROI —you're pulling out your credit card because they're family.

None of this means pets aren't worth it—they absolutely are. They bring joy, companionship, and structure to life. But they're not a budget-friendly trial run for kids. They're a long-term financial decision in their own right, one that reshapes spending patterns, housing choices, and even retirement savings.

So if you're considering adding a furry family member, treat it like planning for a child: calculate the full cost, set aside savings for emergencies, and be sure it fits into your broader financial goals.

The Price Tag of Parenthood

Let's put a number on it.

According to the Brookings Institution, it costs about $310,605 to raise one child born in 2015 through age 17. That doesn't include college, medical surprises, or helping them buy their first car—or home. That's just the basics. It breaks down to around $18,271 per year, or roughly $1,522 per month.

In the language of this book: $50 per day.

That number doesn't seem terrifying until you realize many adults—especially renters, students, and early-career workers—are already living on less than that. If your daily burn rate is already stretched, adding another human being into the mix doesn't just increase costs—it breaks the math entirely.

Let's do a little comparison:

- Median individual income in the U.S. is around $40,000 per year
- Median household income is about $80,000 per year
- One child = a 22.5% hit to your pre-tax income

That assumes a two-income household. If you're raising a child solo? That percentage shoots up fast. Without external support —family, government aid, or subsidized childcare—single parenting can feel like trying to run a marathon on an empty tank. The math just doesn't work.

Children aren't budget items. But if you ignore the cost, the stress will creep into every corner of your life. It's not indulgent spending that derails most families—it's underestimating what's required just to keep going.

The choice to raise kids might be driven by love. But staying afloat? That's all about logistics.

When the Plan Wasn't the Plan

Not every child arrives with a plan. Some show up in the middle of a career change, a housing transition, or a bad breakup. Some are "oops" babies—unplanned, unexpected, and life-altering. When that happens, the spending doesn't wait for your emotions to catch up.

Suddenly, the financial map you had—if you had one—has to be redrawn in real time. What was once manageable becomes mission-critical: housing, food, childcare, insurance. You go from planning someday to paying today. That's when the system needs to show up—not in judgment, but in support.

Surprise parenthood isn't rare. It's human. And it's one of the clearest reasons why our spending systems should be designed with flexibility, not punishment. Because when a baby arrives, everything changes—ESPECIALLY your cost of living.

What It Looks Like in Real Life

Let's take a hypothetical couple with a household income of $80,000. They bring home around $5,000 a month after taxes. Then their first baby arrives. Here's how their new budget looks:

Monthly Expense	Amount
Rent (2-bedroom)	$2,200
Childcare	$1,400
Groceries	$650
Health Insurance	$450
Diapers & Formula	$200
Utilities & Internet	$250
Total	$5,150

They're already $150 over budget—and that's without debt payments, car costs, savings, or unexpected expenses.

This is the real math that breaks people—not bad decision-making, just bad economics.

And that's the truth so many families run into headfirst. They didn't overspend. They didn't blow money on luxuries. They just… had a baby.

You can't bootstrap your way out of rent. You can't coupon-code your way around childcare. You can't love your way through a shortfall that grows by the day.

This isn't financial failure. It's financial design. It's why so many people are one kid away from crisis.

The Financial Shock of Infancy

The first year hits hard.

Even before you think about school or college or extracurriculars, the baby stage brings its own financial storm. Common costs in year one include:

- Diapers: $70 to $80 per month
- Formula: $150 per month if not breastfeeding
- Baby gear: crib, car seat, stroller, monitor—easily $2,000+
- Pediatric care: out-of-pocket visits, vaccinations, urgent care fees

While baby showers help cover some gear, they don't touch the recurring costs. The daily burn creeps up fast—especially when your income stays the same, but your expenses rise with every diaper, bottle, and sleepless night.

Even the so-called "free" options come with trade-offs. Breastfeeding, for instance, may save money on formula, but it costs in other ways—lost work time, physical recovery, stress, and in many cases, lost wages.
And once money starts draining, it drains fast. The savings you built for emergencies? Gone. The credit cards you swore you'd never carry a balance on? Maxed. The financial stress? Constant —and usually silent.

That's the hidden weight of new parenthood in America. Not just the cost of the child… but the cost of staying afloat while your entire life reorganizes itself around them.

The Diaper Scam

There's a quiet cost in early parenthood that no one really warns you about: diapers. Not just the price—but the timeline.

Back in the 1950s, most American children were potty trained by around 18 months. Today? The average is closer to three years old.
That's not biology. That's business.

The diaper industry has spent decades pushing a narrative of "waiting until they're ready"—a message that sounds gentle and respectful but isn't backed by global norms or much science. In many parts of the world, kids are trained by 12 to 18 months. Some families even use "elimination communication," a culturally-rooted method that skips years of diaper use entirely.

But in the U.S., we've been sold something different.

Longer diaper use means more sales. So they invented pull-ups to extend the timeline. They made bigger sizes. They turned a normal developmental milestone into something vague and endlessly delayed. That's up to 18 extra months of diapers—at 6 to 8 a day, around 30 cents each.

The result?

- Families use thousands more diapers—roughly 2,900 extra per child
- That adds up to $800 to $1,000 in additional diaper and wipe costs
- Landfills fill faster, and sustainability takes a hit

It's not just a parenting issue—it's a business model.

This is what modern spending looks like: softened by marketing, hidden in daily purchases, and wildly profitable for someone else.

Childcare: The Second Rent

In many cities, childcare costs as much as housing. And if that sounds absurd, it's because it is.

The Public Policy Institute of California found that infant care can run up to $30,000 per year depending on the county—rivaling the cost of rent or a mortgage. The National Center for Education Statistics reports that's more than the average in-state tuition at a public university. For parents without a financial cushion, it's often a dealbreaker.

Here's what happens:

- Parents delay having more kids—not because they don't want them, but because they can't afford them
- Women step back from the workforce—not because they lack ambition, but because full-time work after taxes and childcare leaves them with nothing
- Families juggle shifts, trade off childcare, or work nights just to make it all fit

And then comes the burnout.

According to a 2022 report from the American Psychological Association, more than 70 percent of new parents reported symptoms of anxiety or depression—often tied directly to financial stress. That's not just emotional strain. That's economic strain manifesting in people's bodies, minds, and relationships. A mom working the graveyard shift. A dad juggling Lyft rides between diaper changes. These aren't personal failures. They're policy failures—quiet, exhausting, and far too common.

Childcare shouldn't cost more than rent. But in America, it often does. When raising kids becomes a luxury, the economy pays the price long after the baby years are over.

Government Programs That Help

Here's the good news: help exists.

There are real programs—federal, state, and local—that can take the edge off parenting costs. Food, healthcare, housing, tax relief. But most of them are underused. Why?

Because people don't know about them. Or they assume they won't qualify. Or they give up after running into red tape, long waitlists, or a sense of shame.

But here's the thing: these programs aren't charity. They're already paid for—by taxpayers, by your neighbors, and probably by you. These are not handouts. These are entitlements. And yes, that means you're entitled to them.

You're not taking from the system. You are the system.

So if the pressure of parenthood is stretching your budget, your nerves, and your sleep to the limit… don't forget that help is built in. You just have to access it. Here are some of the biggest programs parents should know about:

- WIC (Women, Infants, and Children): Provides nutritious food, breastfeeding support, and referrals to healthcare. Can offset up to $150 a month in food costs.
- SNAP (Supplemental Nutrition Assistance Program): Helps low-income households afford groceries. Scales with income and family size.
- CHIP (Children's Health Insurance Program): Offers free or low-cost health coverage for children in working-class families.

- Head Start and Early Head Start: Free early childhood education, health services, and family support for low-income families.
- Child Tax Credit: Offers up to $2,000 per child in tax relief—and when expanded in 2021, it briefly lifted millions of children out of poverty.
- Section 8 Housing Assistance: Helps with rent, freeing up money for everything from diapers to doctor visits.
- Earned Income Tax Credit (EITC): Provides a significant refund for working families with low to moderate income.

Each one takes time and paperwork. But every dollar saved is a dollar you can put toward breathing room, peace of mind, or simply making it to next month.
This is what a functioning society is supposed to look like—neighbors helping each other, even when you don't see them.

When Help Comes Too Late

Most people don't think they'll need help. Not at first.

They have jobs. They budget. They plan. Maybe one partner works full-time while the other covers evenings and weekends. It's tight, but it works—until the baby arrives.

Then daycare hits. Suddenly $1,300 a month is gone before the first diaper box is empty. One parent quits to stay home. Income drops. Rent doesn't.

By the time they realize they qualify for WIC, SNAP, and CHIP, they're already behind. The earliest available appointment is three weeks out. But the lease won't wait. The bills don't pause. The math breaks.

And that delay costs more than just stress. It adds real financial damage:

- One month without WIC = $150 in lost food benefits
- One missed rent payment = $75 to $150 in late fees
- One bounced utility = $35 to $60 in reconnection charges
- One overdraft = $30 to $40 per hit, often compounding

These aren't just frustrating fees. They're daily penalties for falling behind—even temporarily. Once the cycle starts, it pulls people deeper.

So they move in with family. One parent stays out of the workforce. The stress lingers. Not because they made poor choices—but because the support system waited too long to show up.

This isn't unusual. It's exactly what happens when help exists on paper... but not in time.

We don't fail because families don't try. We fail because we design systems that don't act until after the damage is done.

We pay the price for that failure every day—in late fees, lost wages, and lives that spiral not from overspending, but from under-supporting.

Why You Should Care, Even Without Kids

Even if you never plan to raise children, you should care deeply about how we treat the people who do.

Because this isn't just about personal choice—it's about national survival.

If you've ever had pets, you already understand a slice of this pressure. I pay $75 per month per cat just in pet rent. That's $150 a month, or $1,800 a year, before I even buy food, litter, or pay for a vet visit. Toss in food and routine care, and it's easily $3,000 to $4,000 annually to responsibly care for two cats.

Children grow into workers, voters, caregivers, taxpayers, innovators. They are the future labor force that will build bridges, teach classes, serve meals, and pay into Social Security. If we make parenthood financially impossible, we shrink the future.

A falling birthrate might sound like a statistic. But it hits everything—economic growth, home values, retirement systems, even national security.

And the kids who do get raised in poverty? They cost the system more in the long run—through higher healthcare needs, lower lifetime earnings, more housing instability, and missed potential across the board.
Subsidized childcare, tax relief, and parental support aren't luxury policies. They're basic investments in national infrastructure. Just like roads. Just like water.
When we make it easier to raise the next generation, everyone benefits—even those who never change a diaper.

Other Paths: Adoption and Surrogacy

Not everyone takes the biological route. But adoption and surrogacy are just as real, just as beautiful, and often far more expensive.

For many people—queer couples, single parents, people with fertility struggles—these paths aren't optional. They're the only options. But even then, love has to fight through paperwork, delays, and a financial system that seems determined to make family-building feel exclusive.

Here's what it can cost:

- Adoption: $10,000 to $40,000 depending on the type and the state
- Surrogacy: Often exceeds $100,000 when you include medical, legal, and agency fees
- Both routes come with intense emotional labor, legal uncertainty, and long wait times

That's for people who can afford to start the process. For everyone else, the door never opens.

Some companies offer support—especially large firms in tech, finance, or healthcare. A growing number now provide fertility benefits, surrogacy stipends, or paid leave for adoptive parents. These benefits can offset a chunk of the cost—but they're not standard. Access depends heavily on where you work, what insurance you have, and whether your HR department sees family-building as part of employee well-being.

There are also some government supports:

- The federal adoption tax credit can offset up to $15,000 in qualified adoption expenses
- Some states provide subsidies for adopting children from foster care
- Military families may qualify for reimbursement programs or leave options

But these supports require time, research, and paperwork—and they rarely cover everything.

For me, adoption isn't just a distant concept. It's something I've envisioned for my own future—raising siblings from the foster system alongside a child through surrogacy. Not because it's noble. Because it's how I see family: built through love and logistics.

But those logistics? They're brutal. Even well-prepared parents with steady income and clear plans get buried under red tape and rising costs.

The barriers aren't just financial. They're structural. We can't talk about the cost of raising children in this country without talking about how many people are blocked from starting a family at all.

Fixing a Broken Adoption System

Right now, more than 117,000 children in foster care are eligible for adoption.

They're not waiting because no one wants them. They're waiting because the system is slow, fragmented, and underfunded. Every delay comes with a cost—financial, emotional, and structural.

Here's what those delays actually look like:

- Children bounce between temporary placements, often losing trust and stability
- Families walk away mid-process, worn out by the bureaucracy
- Legal fees, home studies, and background checks stack up
- Caseworkers burn out, leaving gaps in communication and follow-through
- Kids age out at 18—alone, unsupported, and without a permanent home

Every one of those outcomes bleeds money.

- Each year a child remains in foster care costs the state between $25,000 and $50,000—more than a year of public college
- Families pay thousands more in legal and travel costs as delays drag on
- The average adoption from foster care takes over three years—time that racks up court fees, home re-certifications, and case management hours
- Kids who age out without a family face higher risks of homelessness, unemployment, and incarceration—all expensive outcomes the state ends up funding anyway

We're not saving money by moving slow. We're spending more to do less.

Adoption isn't just emotionally hard. It's financially rigged. If we streamlined the process—digitized it, coordinated it nationally, prioritized kids over paperwork—we could cut both public costs and private barriers.

It wouldn't take a revolution. It would take a reallocation.

We already spend billions on child welfare. We just spend it too late—and in all the wrong places.

A Shared Responsibility: The Advocacy We All Need

Not everyone can adopt. Not everyone wants to. But if you care about spending smarter, building stronger communities, or giving kids a real shot—you should care deeply about how adoption works in this country.

This isn't just a personal issue. It's public money. It's fiscal policy.

When adoption works, everyone wins:

- Kids get stable homes
- Families get to build a future
- The system stops bleeding money into temporary care
- Taxpayers stop funding inefficiency and abandonment

And when it doesn't? We all pay for that, too.

Every child who ages out of foster care costs the system more—through public housing, emergency services, mental healthcare, and lost economic potential. Over a lifetime, the public cost of one failed placement can exceed $300,000.

So even if you never adopt, you're already part of the equation. You're funding the consequences.

Wouldn't it make more sense to fund the solution?

These are the organizations doing real work—through advocacy, reform, and direct family support:

- Voice for Adoption (VFA): Advocates for foster youth permanency at the federal level
- Dave Thomas Foundation for Adoption: Runs "Wendy's Wonderful Kids," a model focused on finding adoptive homes for children most often overlooked
- Congressional Coalition on Adoption Institute (CCAI): Educates lawmakers and pushes for better legislation
- Families Rising: Supports adoptive families, kinship caregivers, and systemic policy change
- AdoptUSKids: Maintains a national database connecting children with prospective families

This isn't charity. This is infrastructure. This is cost avoidance. If we're serious about reducing poverty, stabilizing communities, and spending our tax dollars wisely, then we have to stop making family-building harder than it has to be.

What Other Countries Get Right

In Sweden, parents get 480 days of paid parental leave—split between both caregivers.

In Germany, childcare is free or heavily subsidized, and many families pay less than $200 a month.

In Canada, universal child benefits offset up to $7,000 a year per child. Poverty rates drop. Educational outcomes rise. And parents aren't forced to choose between income and bonding with their baby.

These aren't radical policies. They're financial infrastructure. Modern, market-based democracies investing in their people the same way they invest in roads, energy, and national defense.

They're not going bankrupt for doing it. These countries still grow businesses, collect taxes, and balance budgets. But they do it with less burnout and more stability.

Even with these benefits, many of these countries still face declining birthrates. But they aren't asking families to bankrupt themselves just to have a child.

And it's not just families who benefit—it's businesses, too. Paid leave, subsidized childcare, and universal healthcare create employees who are more reliable, less stressed, and more likely to return to work. That means:

- Lower turnover
- Fewer unplanned absences
- Better performance and retention
- Less reliance on short-term disability or emergency support programs

Family-forward policies don't just make life easier—they make workplaces stronger. They reduce chaos, increase continuity, and drive long-term savings.

In short: spending on families pays off. At work. At home. Across the economy.

In the U.S., we've taken a different approach. We've privatized reproduction.

Having kids is treated like a lifestyle upgrade—like buying a boat or remodeling a kitchen. Because of that framing, most public support feels optional, limited, or conditional.

Parenthood in America isn't just expensive. It's isolating. Until we shift how we spend as a country, families will keep carrying costs they were never meant to shoulder alone—while businesses keep absorbing the hidden price of national neglect.

What We Could Fix Tomorrow

If we actually wanted to make parenting more affordable—and reduce poverty in the process—we wouldn't have to reinvent the wheel. We'd just have to reallocate.

We already spend billions reacting to crisis. We could spend far less preventing it.

Here's what would move the needle right now:

- Make the Child Tax Credit fully refundable and permanent. In 2021, the expanded version lifted 3 million kids out of poverty. Then we let it expire. That's a choice —not a budget constraint.
- Cap childcare expenses at 7 percent of household income. That's what the federal government already defines as "affordable." It's time to make that a reality, not just a definition.
- Fund universal preschool. This isn't just about education —it's about economic access. Free preschool reduces childcare costs, improves outcomes, and allows more parents—especially mothers—to rejoin the workforce.
- Expand paid family leave. Only 23 percent of U.S. workers have access to paid family leave. We are the only wealthy nation that doesn't mandate it.
- Streamline the adoption process. A coordinated national system could cut wait times, reduce legal fees, and help more families say yes. Right now, too many walk away simply because the process is a mess.
- Subsidize public surrogacy and guardianship programs. If we're serious about equity, we need to support non-traditional family structures—especially for queer parents, single parents, and working-class households who are locked out of the current system.

These aren't radical policies. They're catch-up policies.

They don't just help families—they reduce long-term spending. They prevent homelessness, lower healthcare costs, reduce burnout, and build a stronger tax base for decades to come.

This is the kind of spending that pays for itself. But only if we're willing to invest early, instead of cleaning up late.

Plan with Heart and Math

You'll never feel fully ready. But you can be prepared.

You don't need a perfect nursery or fancy gear. You need a budget. A village. A few programs. A backup plan. And the courage to ask for help when the costs pile up faster than expected.

Don't have kids because you can afford them. Have kids because you love them—and because you've built a system that gives them a real shot at stability.
That system doesn't have to be fancy. It just has to be clear:

- Know your burn rate.
- Know what help is available.
- Know that a $50/day cost doesn't have to break you—if you've mapped it out ahead of time.

A good plan isn't perfect. It's flexible. It leaves room for joy and for chaos, for daycare hiccups and diaper blowouts, for medical bills and messy mornings.

Even if your child wasn't "planned"—your spending still can be. You can adjust. You can get help. You can pivot.

The cost is high. The reward is higher. And with the right policies, the right tools, and the right conversations—we could make parenting feel possible again.

And for those of us raising pets instead of kids, the same truth applies: we made care expensive when it didn't have to be.

Because this doesn't have to be so hard.

We made it hard.
We can make it easier.

Chapter 15: Relationships & Shared Spending

Money doesn't just affect relationships—it reshapes them. It's consistently ranked as the second leading cause of divorce in the U.S., just behind infidelity. That shouldn't surprise us. Because while money looks like math, it behaves like emotion. It carries shame, pride, fear, love… all tangled up in dollars and decisions.

But here's the twist: money doesn't have to be the reason a relationship breaks. It can be the reason it deepens. Talking about money—openly and early—can strengthen trust, build shared goals, and create a deeper kind of intimacy. The kind that's built on truth, not just attraction.

Think about the most important person in your life—or at least the one you talk to most. You probably know what they're doing this weekend. You might know which coworker they're fed up with, what show they're watching, or where they're hoping to travel next.
But do you know what their bank account looks like?
Do they know yours?
Do you know if they're stressed… or silently falling behind?
Do they know what you're saving for—or what's keeping you up at night?

If the answer is no, then you don't really know each other. Not fully. Financial intimacy isn't about spreadsheets. It's about understanding what gives someone stability… and what shakes their foundation. It's about knowing what they're building—or what they're trying to outrun.

Transparency Builds Trust, Not Weakness

Transparency always comes at a cost. You're opening the door to judgment, vulnerability, maybe even rejection. But that door also lets the light in. It's how you build something real.

As a man, I'll be honest—we're not raised to be transparent. We're taught to power through, keep quiet, be the solution. But that kind of stoicism turns into isolation. And isolation kills connection.

Financial transparency is a place to start. It's concrete. It's trackable. It's often easier to say, "I'm $200 short this month" than "I'm scared." But one leads to the other. When you talk about money honestly, other truths follow. Guilt. Shame. Pride. Gratitude.

I've always found it easier to open up about my finances than my feelings—but the two are deeply linked. Some of the best conversations I've had started with a simple "Here's where I'm at… what would you do?" It made money planning feel less like a burden and more like a shared project. Every time, it's drawn people closer—not pushed them away.

Friendships and Financial Generosity

Financial openness isn't just for romantic partners. It matters in friendships too. If your friends are part of your chosen family—and many are—then money should be part of the conversation. Not in a transactional way. In a human way.

When my friends have been between jobs or clearly earning less, I've picked up the tab without blinking. Not because I'm trying to flex. Not because I expect anything back. But because I value their time. And time is the real luxury good.
A $20 lunch in exchange for two hours of laughter, venting, and closeness? That's a steal.

If you're in a position to be generous, be generous. If you're not
—be honest. You might have friends or family who'd help, but
they won't offer unless they know you're struggling. You have
to open the door, even just a crack.

That doesn't mean you start showing up empty-handed or
relying on them every week. Generosity shouldn't be taken for
granted. But transparency lets people show up for you—and
lets you show up for them.

Now let's be real: not everyone rolls like this. You might have a
friend who Venmos you $1.73 for their half of a gas station
Gatorade. That's fine. That's just their financial love language.
The key is alignment, not matching. If your people are
generous, be generous back. If they're strict, respect their rules.
Just don't keep score—and don't go to the well too often.

Because generosity is like credit: the more you borrow without a
plan to repay—financially or emotionally—the faster the
balance turns into resentment.

Economists have a term for this: the free rider problem. It's
when someone benefits from a shared resource without
contributing their fair share. Like the classic dinner example—
nine friends order sandwiches, one person orders lobster, and
everyone splits the bill evenly. At first, it's awkward. Then it
becomes a pattern. And eventually, people stop showing up.
Not because they're cheap—but because they're tired of getting
played.

Financial fairness isn't about equality—it's about respect. If
someone covers you out of love, honor that. And if you're the
one footing the bill, do it from a place of joy—not obligation.
Because the second resentment enters the equation, the
relationship starts to overdraft.

Don't Merge — Coordinate

Let's talk about the real stuff—shared life, shared space, shared bills. When you move in with someone, it makes sense to combine finances... but not in the way most people assume.

The default for a lot of couples is to merge everything. One account. One pool. One big blur of who spent what. But I'd urge you to rethink that—unless one of you is a full-time stay-at-home partner.

Because love is about trust, not entanglement. Merging too fast can actually make things harder to talk about. You lose track of who's contributing what. You start to tiptoe around purchases. If the relationship hits turbulence, unwinding a fully merged financial life is brutal.

That's why I believe in coordination over consolidation. You each keep your own accounts. You each stay financially autonomous. But you build shared systems on top of that—starting with one joint account used only for shared expenses.

That's it. One joint account for the stuff you both benefit from—like rent, groceries, and utilities. Everything else? Stay separate.

This isn't about avoiding commitment. It's about protecting transparency. You can still be "all in" without giving up your financial voice. In fact, keeping part of your financial life separate often helps the conversations get clearer, not harder. It gives you both space—and responsibility.

The Proportional Split: A Partnership Model

Once you've agreed to use a joint account for shared expenses, the next question is: who contributes how much?

Most people default to a 50/50 split. But that only works if you earn the same—which most couples don't. A "fair" split isn't always equal. It's proportional.

Here's how it works:

- One partner makes $40,000
- The other makes $60,000
- That's a 40/60 income split

Now say your shared monthly expenses are:

- $2,000 for rent
- $200 for utilities
- $300 for food
- ➡ = $2,500 total

Partner A pays $1,000. Partner B pays $1,500. That means each person contributes 30% of their income. Different dollar amounts—same effort.

Partner	Income	Contribution %	Monthly Shared Contribution
A	$40,000	40%	$1,000
B	$60,000	60%	$1,500

This model gives you fairness and freedom. You still have personal money to buy gifts, pursue hobbies, or just keep a little breathing room. You're working together, not dissolving your individuality.

Want to save for something big—like a $5,000 vacation? Use the same percentage split. One person contributes $2,000, the other contributes $3,000. That could look like $400 and $600 a month… or $200 and $300 every two weeks, aligned with your paychecks.

Equal effort. Unequal dollars. Shared goals. That's what partnership feels like.

Financial Infidelity Is Still Infidelity

Let's talk about something that doesn't always show up in wedding vows, but absolutely shows up in breakups: hidden money.

Financial infidelity is when one person hides spending, debt, or accounts from the other. And it's way more common than you think. According to a 2023 study by the National Endowment for Financial Education, 43% of adults who share money with a partner admit to doing it. Nearly half.

Some of that is intentional secrecy. But just as often, it's the absence of conversation. A partner who feels stressed spends impulsively. A partner who earns less avoids asking for help. A partner with debt is too ashamed to bring it up. It doesn't always look like lying. But it feels like distance.

I've seen couples in financial crisis—and the real issue wasn't always the money. It was the silence. The Amazon boxes, the takeout, the "Don't worry about it" shrug when things got tight. The longer that silence stretched, the harder it became to fix.

You don't have to sit down every week and read each other's credit card statements like a crime scene. But you do need alignment. Talk monthly. Check in. Ask:

- Are we saving toward something?
- Are we spending in ways we both believe in?
- Is there anything financial that's stressing you out— quietly?

You're not just building a budget. You're building a future. And secrets, even small ones, turn into cracks.

Emotional Honesty and the Cost of Silence

Not every financial betrayal involves hiding a purchase. Sometimes, the damage comes from not saying anything at all.

According to a 2022 U.S. Bank study, more than 30% of couples avoid talking about money entirely—until there's a crisis. By that point, you're not just facing a financial problem. You're facing a communication breakdown.
Plenty of couples split bills evenly, save responsibly, and plan vacations—on paper, they're doing everything right. But when the emotional side of money goes unspoken, cracks start to form.

Maybe one person starts to feel anxious about work or guilty about a recent expense. Maybe there's a creeping sense that the financial balance isn't fair anymore. But instead of having that hard conversation, they let it fester. They stay silent.

That silence builds tension. One partner might want to save for a home, while the other keeps buying gadgets—not recklessly, just regularly. Without a shared vision, those small choices start to feel like misalignment.

Or maybe one partner earns less and quietly feels like they're not contributing enough. Instead of speaking up, they overcompensate—splurging on gifts, refusing help, or burying the stress under pride.

The issue isn't just the money. It's the unspoken feelings behind it.

Financial silence becomes emotional noise. It creates distance. It fosters resentment. Even in otherwise healthy relationships. And no—this isn't about telling your partner every time you grab a #1 at your favorite fast food place. It's about the big picture. The stress that's building. The goals that feel lopsided. The stuff that shapes the future, not just the receipt.

That's why financial intimacy matters. Not to micromanage each other—but to stay connected. Ask:

- What does fairness look like to both of us?
- Are we each carrying what we can?
- Are we aligned on what we're building together—or just avoiding a tough talk?

The truth is, money won't ruin your relationship. But avoiding the truth about money just might.

Your Network Can Be a Safety Net

Not all help comes from systems or strangers. Sometimes, it comes from the people right in front of you. Friends. Siblings. Parents. Even a roommate.

If you're struggling—whether it's debt, job loss, or just a rough patch—they might be able to help. But only if they know. Transparency is the doorway to support.

I'm not talking about meals or spot covers—that kind of generosity lives in day-to-day friendship. I'm talking about the big stuff. The moments when a single check or short-term loan could change your whole financial trajectory.

The IRS allows up to $19,000 per year in tax-free gifts. That's enough to help someone wipe out a credit card or move into a safer apartment. But gifts like that need structure. Not paperwork, necessarily—but clarity.

If you offer support, make expectations known. Is it a gift? A loan? A one-time thing?

If you receive support, communicate. Show how it's helping. Set a timeline if repayment is part of the plan. Express gratitude clearly and consistently.

These aren't just transactions. They're relationships. Money doesn't just fix things—it can strain them. So treat help as a bridge, not a blank check.

Because when money shows up without communication, resentment often sneaks in right behind it.

Build Toward Shared Vision

Love is not a financial strategy. But your financial strategy says a lot about how you love.

Because shared spending isn't just about who pays for what. It's about what you value, what you're building, and whether you're actually building it together.

The people closest to you deserve more than just honesty about your income. They deserve to know what you're dreaming about. What you're afraid of. What you're hoping to create.

They deserve to be part of that vision—if you're choosing to build one with them.

So talk early. Talk often. Don't wait for the resentment to pile up or the numbers to stop making sense.

Money doesn't need to be a landmine. It can be a map. A shared one. A tool for clarity, not control.

Because at the end of the day, it's not a joint account that builds a future.

It's a joint vision.

Chapter 16: Big Purchases & Value Thinking

L et me introduce you to something I like to call the Video Game Index.

It's not scientific—but it works. If something costs as much as a video game system—whether that's a Nintendo Switch Lite, Xbox, Steam Deck or a PS5—you owe it to yourself to pause. Not forever. Just long enough to ask:

- How long will this set me back?
- How many hours would I need to work to afford this—after taxes?
- Will this throw off any plans, savings goals, or financial momentum?

At that price point—somewhere between $200 and $500—a purchase starts to matter. It might not wreck your budget, but it can quietly slow you down. Slowing down matters. Because money builds momentum. Every dollar you redirect toward something you don't really need is a dollar that could've been fueling the life you actually want.

That's the power of the Video Game Index. It's not about guilt—it's about creating a personal threshold. A number that forces you to stop and think. For me, it's the cost of a video game console. For you, it might be a concert ticket, a handbag, or even a grocery delivery habit that adds up fast. But once you define that line, you start protecting yourself from impulsive decisions disguised as needs.

And that pause? It's everything.

Most big purchases aren't emergencies. Even *some* medical ones. I've broken my wrists three times—left in 2nd grade, right in middle school, and left again two years ago when I got a plate put in. Even then, I wasn't rushed into surgery. I had nearly a week to weigh options, ask questions, and make a plan. That's about as high-stakes as it gets.

But compare that to what happens when your car breaks down on a Monday morning. People panic. They rush to the dealership that afternoon. And by dinner, they're $40,000 in debt—without researching, comparing, or negotiating.

You could've taken a rideshare for a week. Even at $50 a day, that's $350—not $40,000.
But urgency plays tricks on you. It makes temporary fixes feel impossible… and permanent decisions feel necessary.

You deserve better planning than that.

Used Doesn't Mean Lesser—It Means Smarter

One of the most powerful financial decisions you can make is to need less. But the second most powerful? Reframing what "new" even means.

If you're going to be frugal—be frugal with purpose. Buying used doesn't just save money. It keeps things out of landfills. It softens your footprint. And it disrupts the endless cycle of marketing that tells you shiny and fresh is the only kind of status.

My philosophy is simple: Buy once—and if you can, buy secondhand.
Thrift stores, used furniture outlets, refurbished tech… all of it gets you 90% of the function for 30% of the cost. More importantly, it breaks the pattern of waste. Especially when buying cheap usually means replacing often.

So if you're going to be "cheap," do it with intention.
Be the person who values durability, not packaging. Be the person who sees beauty in reuse, not just retail.

The best savings aren't always measured in dollars.
Sometimes, it's knowing you didn't fall for the marketing that
says newer means better.

Buying secondhand is one way to stay ahead of the hidden
costs. But what really matters is recognizing those costs in the
first place—especially when they're dressed up as something
you "deserve."
Because some of the most expensive choices don't feel like
mistakes when you make them.
They feel like progress. Like status. Like success.

Until they don't.

The Real Cost of the Things You "Deserve"

Let's talk about total cost of ownership—or as I like to call it, the
invisible price tag. It's the part no one tells you about in the ad.
The costs that show up later… when the excitement fades and
the invoices roll in.

I once upgraded from a basic domestic car to a sleek European
import. On the surface, it felt like progress. Like I had "leveled
up." But under the hood—financially and emotionally—it
became a drain.

Here's what happened:

- My oil changes jumped from $100 to over $600.
- Repairs routinely crossed $1,000.
- One standard fix came back with a $3,000 estimate.
- And it required premium gas—another small, relentless
  bleed.

At first, I told myself I deserved it. That it was a reward. But
slowly, that pride turned into frustration. I started to resent the
car. Every dashboard light felt like a threat. Every unexpected
expense chipped away at my peace. It wasn't just money—it

was energy. Regret. And a quiet voice asking, "Why did I do this?"

We talk a lot about budgeting for the price tag. But what about the cost of emotional maintenance? The stress? The second-guessing? The shame that comes from knowing you chose something that doesn't fit your life?

The wrong purchase doesn't just drain your bank account—it drains your clarity. And that erosion? It spreads.

This mindset applies to housing, too. You might think buying a home is the "grown-up" move. That renting is throwing money away. But it's not that simple.

When you rent, someone else handles the roof leak, the plumbing nightmare, the busted AC in August. When you own, those costs—and that stress—become yours. And they never arrive when you're ready.

Let's not forget:

- Property taxes that increase year over year
- HOA fees that feel like a second rent
- Surprise maintenance that always shows up during the worst week
- The pressure to furnish and upgrade "that extra room" you don't use

Owning a home can be great—if you're truly ready. But buying just because "you're supposed to"? That's not maturity. That's marketing. And it's one of the most expensive traps people fall into.

Luxury vs. Value – Know the Difference

There's a difference between luxury and value—and it's not about price.

Value means something is worth it. It lasts. It works. It fits your life.
Luxury often means it's priced above its utility—but dressed in status, scarcity, or experience.

Here's a silly but real example: the Costco hot dog.
$1.50. Tastes solid. No surprises. An absolute win.
Now compare that to the $10... or even $15... hot dog at a stadium. Same calories. Same paper wrapper. Very different vibe.

At the stadium, you're not paying for food. You're paying for the moment. And that's fine. That's what luxury is: context-dependent value.
But you have to be honest with yourself. Don't pretend it's practical. Don't call it necessary. Just call it what it is—a splurge. And splurges are fine. But only when they fit into the bigger plan.

Here's a more serious example:

A friend of mine was considering a BMW X1. It looked great. She worked from home and only drove about 20 minutes a day —10 there, 10 back. I asked her one simple question:

"Will this car help you take more trips with your kids—or take trips away from them?"

Because that's what it was. A trade.

And every big purchase is a trade. Of time. Of money. Of future options.

She's not alone. According to AAA, the average total cost of owning and operating a new car in 2023 was over $12,000 a year —or about $1,015 per month. That includes everything: gas, insurance, maintenance, depreciation, loan interest, and fees. It's not extra on top of the car—it is the cost of using the car.

For many people, that's more than their rent. But we treat it like a given. Because no one wants to feel like they've downgraded... even when their finances are quietly begging them to.

But if your car is eating your future, it's not an upgrade. It's a leash.

This is where so many people fall behind.
You're not just buying the thing—you're trading what comes next for it.
Sometimes that's worth it. Most of the time... it's not.

Let's Kill the $5 Coffee Myth

You've probably heard someone say,
"If you stopped buying that $5 coffee every day, you could afford a house."

No, you couldn't.

At $5 a day, that's about $1,825 a year. Not nothing. But it's not a down payment—not in this housing market. Not with interest rates where they are. Not after decades of policy decisions that hollowed out the middle class and inflated the cost of living.

And that's what makes this myth so frustrating.
It doesn't just miss the point—it blames the wrong people.

Millennials and the generations that followed didn't create wage stagnation, runaway housing costs, or predatory lending. We inherited them.
And now we're being told the problem is a cup of coffee we actually enjoy?
Come on.

The real issue isn't the coffee.

It's the $2,000 car upgrade… plus the $3,000 vacation on a credit card… plus the $400 impulse splurge from a targeted ad.
It's not about one habit.
It's about stacked habits, left unexamined. And that happens when life already feels out of control.

But small changes can make a difference—when they're intentional.

I bought a nice coffee maker a few years ago. It cost about $300. Since then, my daily coffee costs maybe $1. I still drink great coffee every morning. But I'm spending $1,300 less a year doing it.

That's the point.

The goal isn't to strip joy from your life. It's to make sure joy isn't costing you your future. That's the sweet spot—comfort, quality, and efficiency, all working together.

This is also why Buy Now, Pay Later services have exploded. Especially for purchases under $1,000. Since 2020, usage has more than doubled. Because the pressure point isn't $10,000 loans anymore. It's the $400 splurge disguised as a "manageable" monthly charge.

The illusion of affordability is powerful—especially when it's broken into payments, dressed in zero-interest marketing, and dropped into your cart with a single click.

Subscription Creep: When "Small" Costs Go Big

Here's a category of spending that hides in plain sight: big-ticket subscriptions.

You might think, "It's only $30/month," but multiply that by five or six platforms, and you're suddenly spending $200–$400/month without realizing it. Studies show that most people underestimate their subscription spending by two to three times, with the average household spending over $300 per month — often on things they barely use. That's over $3,600 a year — a round-trip vacation or a credit card payoff, quietly disappearing in monthly increments.

Here's where it gets dangerous:

- Meal kits can run you $400–$600/month
- Boutique gyms? $150–$300/month
- Streaming bundles with every add-on? Another $80+
- Premium app stacks, cloud storage, news sites, coaching apps…

If you're making six figures, maybe you can carry those comfortably. But most people can't. They're bleeding out through what feels like small holes — but those holes are everywhere.

And let's be honest: you're not watching all of it. You're not using all of it. You're paying for convenience, comfort, and the illusion of improvement.

That's fine… if you can afford it. But ask yourself:

- If this was billed as a one-time annual charge, would I still say yes?
- Do I even remember signing up?
- Have I used this in the last 30 days?

If the answer is no, cancel it today. No guilt. Just clarity.

The 30-Day Rule — and the Power of Patience

Let's say you want to buy something big. A laptop. A sofa. A vacation. Whatever it is… wait 30 days.

Seriously—just wait.

Because urgency is almost always manufactured.

Marketers are trained to make you feel like your life will be incomplete without it. That if you don't buy now, you'll miss out.

But here's the truth: if something is truly valuable, it'll still be valuable in 30 days.

Here's what happens when you wait:

- You get clarity on whether you actually need it
- You learn whether it was emotional impulse or real utility
- You often realize the excitement fades—and that's your answer

Even better? Save up for it. When you have the money in hand, something powerful happens:

You now have a second decision point—

"Do I still want to part with this cash now that it's mine?"

That pause—that space between want and buy—is where financial maturity lives.

It's not about guilt. It's about power. Control. Freedom.

As of 2024, the average American carried over $6,000 in credit card debt. And much of it didn't come from emergencies. It came from purchases like:

- Clothes bought for a confidence boost
- Furniture bought to impress someone
- Trips taken on a whim
- In some cases, financing for cars that were more about image than need

These weren't reckless decisions—they were emotional ones. They felt justified in the moment… but became burdens over time.

When you build in delay, you protect yourself from that spiral.

You make space for the truth to catch up to the feeling.
And nine times out of ten, the truth is this: you didn't need it.
You just needed time.

Before You Swipe, Ask...

Here's your gut-check.

Before you swipe, tap, or click "Buy Now," take 30 seconds and ask:

- How long will this take to pay off?
- What's the full cost over time—maintenance, storage, upgrades, insurance?
- Is there a version that's 80% as good for 50% the cost?
- Am I buying this for me—or for someone else's approval?
- What will I have to give up in order to afford this?
- If I wait 30 days, will I still want it?

Big purchases don't just spend money—they spend momentum. And if you're not careful, they'll stall your progress before you even realize you've veered off course.

So pause.
Wait.
Think.

And if it still feels right—buy it.

Just make sure what you're gaining is worth more than what you're giving up.
Because every dollar is a decision...
and your future is built one choice at a time.

But not every decision is big and obvious. Some are tiny, quiet, recurring choices you barely notice—until you realize they've been draining you for months.

Chapter 17: Subscription Culture & Sludge

There is nothing closer to me than subscription culture and sludge.

Take it from a retired cable guy who spent over 15 years watching entire industries perfect the art of keeping you just interested enough not to cancel. That slowdown you experience when you try to leave a service? That's not a glitch. That's sludge.

You saw it during the pandemic—people stuck paying $10 a month for Planet Fitness because the only way to cancel was in person. During COVID. Before we even knew how it spread. People were scared... and they just let the charge ride.

That's sludge.

It's not laziness. It's friction. It's on purpose. Designed to keep the status quo in place—and your wallet open.

If Taco Bell can take your order and have you back on the road in five minutes, then streaming services, internet providers, and gyms should be able to cancel your membership just as fast.
But many don't.
Because friction is profitable—and slowing you down is part of the plan.

The Rule That Almost Was

We came close to real progress.

In 2021, the Federal Trade Commission proposed a rule called "Click to Cancel" under the Restore Online Shoppers' Confidence Act (ROSCA).

It would've required companies to let you cancel a subscription the same way you signed up. Sign up online? Cancel online. Seems obvious, right?

But the rule stalled—like so many consumer protections—because we didn't vote for the folks who would've made it law. Just like that, it faded into the stack of good ideas that never got through.

So now we operate in the world we have… not the world we want.

But that doesn't mean we're powerless.
It just means we need to get intentional.

Take Inventory — Now

Let's get practical.

Start by asking: how many subscriptions do you actually have?

Check your credit card statements. Or use a tool like Rocket Money or Trim. The average household has at least four streaming services—and that's just for content.

Netflix. Hulu. Amazon Prime. Disney+. Apple TV. Maybe a bundle deal that seemed like a steal.
$15 here. $12 there. $25 for the "premium" tier. It adds up—fast.

Those are the obvious ones.

Now think about the quiet charges:

- The gym you haven't visited since January
- The cable package you "keep for football"
- The meal kit you swore you'd cancel last month
- The meditation app you keep out of guilt

That's all sludge. That's all waste.
It's not an accident—it's a business model.

Two Strategies to Regain Control

So how do you fight back?

Start with two simple rules:

1. Treat every subscription like a trial.
   Sign up. Use it. Then cancel. If it's worth keeping,
   you'll know. But this forces you to be intentional, not
   passive.
2. Always check the tier.
   I once paid for the premium Chuze Fitness plan
   because it came with massage chairs and access to
   other locations. Sounds nice. But I never used either.
   Not once.

That year? $240, gone. For nothing.

Same goes for content.
If you only watch one show on Disney+, cancel. Come back
when the season's over. Watch it all in a month and move on.
You're not quitting—you're rotating.

That's the mindset shift: you're not missing out. You're making
space for better choices.

The Psychology of "Just One More"

Let's zoom in on how subscriptions are designed to bypass your
defenses.

You're not just being offered a service—you're being trained.
Every free trial. Every auto-renew. Every "$1 to start" promo.
It's all aimed at one thing: getting you to say yes once… and
never stop.

Because once you say yes, inertia takes over.
It's easier to let things ride than to make a decision.

Especially when the price is low.
$5… $9… $14 a month? Most people don't even pause. You see
the charge, you shrug, and say, "It's not that bad."

But that's the trap.
Not bad enough to cancel.
Not good enough to care.
It just lingers.

Multiply that by ten or fifteen services and suddenly you're
spending $150–$250 every month—without realizing it.

That's not overspending. That's ambient draining.
And it's not an accident.

Behind the scenes, companies even track this behavior. They call
it LTV drift—lifetime value that grows not because you use the
product, but because you forgot it exists.

It's not about loyalty.
It's about forgetting.

Gamified Spending and the Subscription Illusion

I remember getting an email from Grammarly once that said,
"You used more unique words than 91% of users."

I didn't need that information. It didn't change how I write.
But I opened that email. I felt good for a second. And I kept
going.

Then, after my subscription expired, I got another one:
"You didn't have any writing activity last week. Your streak is
now 0. Sign in to earn your next achievement."

It was basically saying, "You broke your streak… are you okay?"

That's not support. That's strategy. That's gamified shame, wrapped in productivity language.

And Grammarly's not alone.

- Duolingo shames you for missing a lesson.
- Fitness apps track your streaks, hand out badges, and nudge you when you fall behind.
- Language tools, meditation platforms, even budgeting apps—almost all of them dangle "achievements" to keep you locked in.

You're not just subscribing to a service. You're entering a system designed to praise your progress… and punish your absence.

So ask yourself:

Which of your subscriptions are subtly making you feel bad for stopping?

Which ones are using streaks, badges, or artificial milestones to make you stay?

Because when motivation turns into manipulation, it's not encouragement—it's a trap.

That trap is designed to monetize your guilt.

Why We Cling to the Queue

Let's be honest—sometimes we don't cancel because we're afraid of what we'll lose.

Not materially. Emotionally.

That half-finished season.

That playlist you "might" revisit.

That niche documentary you bookmarked during a phase you're no longer in.

It's not about needing the content.
It's about not wanting to feel like you gave something up.

The queue becomes a to-do list.
The gym key tag becomes a badge of intent.
The meal kit becomes a symbol of the version of you that cooks more, plans better, wastes less.

It's not about usage. It's about identity.

That emotional attachment is powerful.
It makes canceling feel like failure—even when it's clearly the right move.

But here's the truth:
You're not falling behind by canceling.
You're catching up—to yourself.

You're making space for what you actually use, value, and enjoy... instead of clinging to what you hoped you might.

The Shopping Subscriptions You Don't Question

Let's talk about the big ones—the subscriptions we don't even think of as subscriptions.

Amazon Prime is the king here.

Prime members spend nearly twice as much as non-members. And Amazon knows it.
At a UCLA conference, one professor even revealed that Amazon could predict your buying behavior based on which shows you're watching—The Marvelous Mrs. Maisel vs. The Boys. Not because of the content. Because of what those preferences say about your spending triggers.

Then there's Costco.
It's just as calculated.

Wandering the warehouse is the point. The layout is designed to
slow you down.
Samples. Seasonal deals. Limited-time offers.
It all creates a sense of momentum that feels like saving… but
often leads to buying more than you planned.
The membership fee? That $65 price tag only feels like a bargain
if you were going to shop there anyway.

Otherwise, it's just another form of sunk-cost logic.
"I have the membership, so I might as well…"
That's not value. That's a nudge disguised as a deal.

Stickiness by Design

In marketing, we used to call it stickiness—the emotional
residue that keeps you from canceling, even when you know
you should.

Autopay. Guilt messaging. Post-purchase upsells.
Even something as small as your saved playlists or workout
history—they're not just features. They're anchors.

That's how companies keep you.

Ask yourself:

Would you really miss your Amazon wishlist?
Probably not—it's still there, membership or not.

But your Netflix queue? Your saved workouts? Your Duolingo
streak?

That's where the trap is.

How to Audit Like a Pro

Let's get tactical.

You don't need a spreadsheet or a finance degree. You just need a system.

Here's how to run a monthly subscription audit:

1. Pull your bank and credit card statements.
   Look for anything recurring—monthly, quarterly, even annual.
2. Label each one:
   Essential (you rely on it)
   Joy-based (you actually use and enjoy it)
   Sludge (you forgot you had it, or you're keeping it out of guilt)
3. Cancel anything you didn't use at least twice last month.
4. Set a hard cap.
   For most people, $100/month on subscriptions is more than enough.
   Add one? Drop one. Rotate. Prioritize.
5. Use reminders.
   If you subscribe to something new, set a calendar alert for 25 days out—so you're not surprised when the trial ends.

This isn't about punishment.
It's about alignment.

You're not budgeting from a place of restriction.
You're setting guardrails to protect your momentum.

Small leaks don't feel dangerous—until they flood everything.

The Math of Time and Use

Let's break it down.

Most shows now run about 8 episodes. That's roughly 8 hours per season.
Seems manageable—until you look at your week.

If you work 9 to 5, add in a commute, meals, chores, and the human need to rest...
You probably have 2 to 3 hours of screen time per night.
That's enough to keep up with one or two shows per week.
Maybe.

But most people are paying for five or six platforms.
You're not using them all—you're storing them, like digital pantry items you'll "get around to."
You're not watching for joy. You're watching to catch up.
You're not choosing. You're juggling.

Here's the worst part?

You're paying for that pressure.

You're paying for guilt. For a queue you'll never finish. For a content library that feels too good to cancel—but too overwhelming to enjoy.

Every week you hold onto a subscription you don't use?
That's another $10–$20 disappearing. Quietly. Automatically.
Multiply that by five platforms, and you're burning through $50 to $100 a month—not on joy, but on indecision.

You're not just wasting time.
You're funding your own overwhelm.

But here's the secret:
You won't miss most of it.

Once it's gone, you'll realize you weren't using it—you were holding onto the idea of using it.

The Hidden Cost of Sludge

Richard Thaler — the Nobel Prize-winning economist — coined the term "sludge" to describe exactly this:
anything that slows you down when you're trying to do something good for yourself.

A few extra clicks. A buried cancellation page.
A "special offer" that makes you second-guess your decision to leave.
It all adds up—not by mistake, but by design.

Companies know what they're doing. They call it breakage—revenue from people who forget to cancel.
That's not a rounding error. That's the business model.

They're not making money when you use the product.
They're making money when you're too tired to stop using it.
It's not about laziness. It's about leverage.
Sludge is how they win the war of attrition—by waiting you out.

That exhaustion has a cost.

You might think it's "just $9.99." But it's not.
Because no one has just one subscription.
That $10 charge is often multiplied across ten or more services—and across months or even years.
It's $300 here, $600 there, maybe $1,200 across a year.
All for things you didn't need… or didn't remember.

Sludge is a hidden tax on the overwhelmed.
The system is rigged to keep it in place.

The Sludge Targeting Your Kids

This isn't just happening to adults.
Sludge shows up in kids' lives too—and often more
aggressively.

Apps like ABCmouse, Prodigy Math, and countless mobile
games hook kids into recurring charges.
Battle passes. Daily bonuses. Monthly unlocks.
All of it plays on the same psychological trick:
Canceling feels like punishment.

Those charges aren't small.
$6.99 here, $14.99 there... some "educational" apps creep up to
$30/month before you notice.
Add in a few game passes and streaming add-ons, and
suddenly you're spending $50 to $100 a month—just to keep the
peace.

Even schools are in on it.
Families are now expected to subscribe to classroom apps,
homework platforms, and online testing tools—often without
much choice.
If you don't, your kid feels left out.
And you feel like a bad parent.

Sludge weaponizes guilt.

It teaches kids that money is friction... and friction is normal.
That canceling something means letting people down.
That the baseline is paid—and the free version is something to
escape from, not something to appreciate.

When that mindset starts early, it sticks.

So if you're a parent, ask yourself:
What are you paying for out of guilt or ease?
Is it worth it?

More importantly…
What is it teaching your kid about money?

Subscriptions should be a conversation—not a trap.

The Retail Subscription Creep

Sludge doesn't stop with media or kids' apps.
It's creeping into every corner of retail life.

- Auto-refills on skincare, vitamins, or supplements you stopped using (think Curology or Ritual)
- Wellness memberships for things like float tanks, cryotherapy, or infrared saunas you "mean to use"
- Meal kits like HelloFresh or Blue Apron that keep delivering even when your schedule doesn't
- Retail memberships like Thrive Market or warehouse clubs you rarely visit
- Shaving kits from brands like Billie or Dollar Shave Club that pile up in your bathroom drawer

These aren't impulse buys.
They're automated charges, engineered to fly under your radar.
They're priced just below your pain point—$9.99, $12.99, maybe $14.99—because that's what most people ignore for months. Or years.
By the time you notice?
You've been paying for months—sometimes years—for things you didn't use… and never really wanted.
That's the power of passive spending.
You don't feel it. But your bank account does.

And the worst part?
It doesn't feel like a mistake.
It feels like maintenance.
Like something you're "supposed" to keep—just in case.

The Hidden Tax on the Overwhelmed

Sludge hits hardest when you're too tired to deal with it.

If you've ever been too exhausted to cancel a subscription—
even one you knew you didn't want—that wasn't laziness. That
was design. The entire point of sludge is to wait you out.

Companies call it "breakage"—the money they make off people
who forget to cancel. That's not a bug in the system. That is the
system.

It works best on people who are stretched thin.

Ever tried to cancel your internet or cable service?
Signing up takes seconds—you're on the phone with a sales rep
in no time.
But the moment you say "cancel," you're transferred. Put on
hold. Told to explain yourself.
Retention takes forever. On purpose.

Who has that kind of time on a Tuesday night after work?

Now imagine doing that for every forgotten charge on your
statement.

This is why the financial literacy conversation can't stop at
budgeting.
Because budgeting assumes you have time. Energy. Capacity.

But the reality is: time poverty creates money poverty.

The people least able to afford $10 mistakes are the ones who
pay for them most often—not because they're irresponsible, but
because they're overwhelmed.

Sludge becomes a hidden tax on the exhausted.
On the caregivers. The overworked. The underpaid.

On the people who need relief most.

That's not personal failure.
That's systemic design.

Why This Isn't Just About You

Here's the truth that cuts deeper: sludge doesn't hit everyone equally.

If you're juggling two jobs, managing stress, raising kids, or just trying to make rent, you're far more likely to miss a $12 charge... or feel too burnt out to argue with a customer service rep.

So who pays the most for corporate friction?

The people with the least time and the fewest resources.

That's not unfortunate. That's intentional.
Because the system isn't designed around fairness. It's designed around friction.
Friction works best when your energy is already gone.

The more overextended you are, the more vulnerable you become to passive charges, renewal traps, and emotional guilt tactics. You spend more—not because you choose to, but because you're too tired to choose anything different.

So this isn't just a personal finance problem.
It's a political one.

It's another way wealth gets extracted—quietly, invisibly, one small charge at a time—from people who are just trying to hold it together.

It adds up.

As of 2023, the average U.S. consumer spent approximately $273 per month on subscription services, according to data from C+R Research. That's over $3,200 per year—much of it unnoticed, unplanned, or unneeded.

Multiply that across 100 million households.
That's hundreds of billions of dollars flowing out of working wallets… and into corporations that bank on your exhaustion.

Fighting sludge isn't just a budgeting tactic.
It's resistance.
It's reclaiming what's yours.

Cancel Boldly. Unsubscribe Without Guilt.

You've been trained not to cancel.
Not to question.
Not to unplug.

But canceling isn't giving up.
It's getting free.

You don't have to stop watching TV.
You don't have to cancel your gym.
You don't have to avoid every service.

You just need to own it.

Know what you're spending.
Know what you're actually using.
Be honest about what adds value—and what just adds noise.

And here's the secret: when you do cancel?
You probably won't miss it.

You won't mourn it.
You won't keep wondering.
You'll just feel lighter.

Canceling is not deprivation.
It's direction.
So log in.
Hit unsubscribe.
Shut it down.

Then sit with what comes next—
a little extra breathing room,
a little more power in your pocket,
and a lot more clarity moving forward.
Escaping the sludge of subscriptions isn't just about saving
money. It's about freeing up something even more valuable—
your time and mental bandwidth.

When you cancel a subscription or automate a passive cost
down to zero, you're not just stopping a financial leak—you're
buying back hours of your life. What you do with that time is
where real ROI begins.

That's why next, we shift from cutting costs to investing them
wisely—not just in markets or retirement accounts, but in
yourself.

Chapter 18: Personal Return on Investment

Return on investment (ROI) is a simple enough concept. You spend $100, and you hope it turns into $150. You want a return—preferably more than you put in. That's the math. But in real life, the math gets messy. The currency isn't always money.

I used to manage a $3.2 million marketing budget at a national telecom company. My job was to track ROI with absolute clarity. If we spent $40,000 on a new mover program, how many customers did it bring in? What was the lifetime value? Could we scale it, cut it, repeat it? ROI was gospel—and we measured everything that way.

But outside of spreadsheets, ROI looks different. What's the return on spending thirty quiet minutes with someone you love instead of diving into your inbox? What's the value of taking a breath instead of taking another meeting? What's the ROI of being well instead of constantly being productive?

In this chapter, we're talking about a different kind of spending. Not just dollars—but time, energy, care, attention, and presence. The finite parts of yourself that get spent every day, whether you realize it or not.

Some of the smartest investments won't make you richer. They'll just make you need less. Less validation. Less numbing. Less urgency to keep chasing something that doesn't feel like peace.

That's the real ROI: not just what you gain, but what you no longer need.
This chapter is about those kinds of returns—how we spend our time, protect our mental bandwidth, and give to others in a way

that builds a life that feels whole... even when no one's watching.

Time – The Only Finite Asset You'll Ever Own

Not all spending shows up on a bank statement. Some of the highest costs in your life will be emotional, not financial. Time is one of them. So is energy. So is belief. The returns aren't measured in dollars—they're measured in direction. In who you become.

Of all the resources you'll ever touch—money, talent, even luck—time is the only one you can't earn back. It's spent, every day, with or without intention. That's why how you spend your time is one of the clearest indicators of what you value... even if it's not what you say you value.

The truth is, time investment rarely pays off right away.

When I got into Syracuse, I wasn't a scholarship recruit. No fanfare. No scouts. But the moment that acceptance letter hit, I made a choice: I was going to spend my time like I belonged on that lacrosse team—even if no one believed I did. So I trained. Hard. Before classes even started. I wasn't waiting for someone to invite me. I was spending the only thing I had: time.

Eventually, I walked onto one of the most competitive Division I programs in the country. A team with 22 straight Final Four appearances. I didn't play, but I made the team. I out-trained the odds. I stayed on that team by spending more time in the gym, more time studying tape, more time grinding when others rested. I wasn't spending time for attention—I was spending it to prove to myself that I could do what they said I couldn't.

Years later, when I applied to business school, I brought the same mindset. I studied five hours a day for months just to make myself competitive for the top programs. I wasn't a polished applicant. I wasn't an early decision. But I invested time like someone who knew what that degree could do. And it worked. Accepted at UCLA Anderson… not too bad for a third-round applicant. The return came—but only after months of spending with no guarantees.

Even then, the early return nearly slipped away. I ended up on academic probation my first two quarters—not because I couldn't keep up, but because I was still living like a college athlete who knew how to party. I had to recalibrate. So I started spending time like someone who wanted to stay in. Three hours a night in the library. Weekends locked in. I found my edge again—by investing time with precision.

I even got strategic. Since grades were curved, I stopped trying to be the best and started influencing the curve itself. "You only have to beat seven people to get a B," I used to say. I lobbied my section every Saturday to aim low enough that I could breathe. It worked. We became the lowest-performing section… and I got off probation.

That part won't make it into any TED Talk. But it's real. It's proof that time, when spent with purpose—whether in the gym, the stacks, or gaming the system—is still spending. It's a cost. If you spend it with intention, it might just change your life.

Therapy – Emotional Health is Real Discipline

If time is your most finite asset, then mental clarity might be your most underrated one.

I've always had an anxious mind. That's not self-deprecating—it's just realism. I'm someone who notices things, connects dots, runs scenarios. I forecast the worst not because I'm negative, but because I want to be prepared. The problem is… that kind of mind never really shuts off. It loops. It spirals. It burns energy even when there's nothing to solve.

That kind of mental pace has a cost—and eventually, I realized I was paying it every day.

Therapy has an upfront cost—sometimes emotional, sometimes financial, often both.

If you're paying out of pocket, it's not cheap. Depending on your area, therapy can run anywhere from $75 to $200+ per session. Even with insurance, co-pays can add up fast. You're not just spending money—you're spending time, energy, and emotional bandwidth.

But there are workarounds. Many companies (like mine at the time) offer 6–10 free sessions a year through their employee benefits programs. Not perfect, but better than nothing. Community clinics, schools, and state programs also offer reduced-cost options if you're willing to ask. Online platforms like BetterHelp or Talkspace can start as low as $60 a week—though with a tradeoff: you may be talking to a different therapist each time, or getting responses that feel templated. You're paying for speed and access, not deep relationship-building.

Even AI tools—like ChatGPT—are entering the space. I use it myself to process thoughts, calm spirals, and prepare for hard conversations. It's become part of my daily mental hygiene. But AI can't hold eye contact. It doesn't notice when your voice cracks. It can't replace the work—it can only reflect it back to you.

And let's be clear: this technology still needs guardrails. A 2025 Time Magazine investigation found that some mental health apps were giving dangerously unfiltered responses—offering advice without context, empathy, or accountability. The risk isn't just that AI gets it wrong. It's that it sounds confident while getting it wrong. Without a human to challenge or clarify, that can spiral fast.

AI can help. But it can't replace human care—at least not yet. You still have to do the real work—and sometimes, that means sitting across from someone who can see what you're not saying.

The first time I went to therapy, I used the eight free sessions my company provided. There was no breakdown. No rock bottom. Just a quiet understanding that I could probably live—and think —a little better.

What opened that door for me wasn't a TED Talk or a podcast. It was The Thomas Crown Affair. Pierce Brosnan's version. A nearly flawless man—cool, calculated, always ahead—and yet he still went to therapy. He still sat down, opened up, processed. The movie never framed it as weakness. It was strength. It was strategy. That stuck with me.

So I gave it a shot—and therapy delivered. Not instant clarity, but real frameworks. I learned how to pause a thought before it spiraled. How to separate feeling from fact. How to notice the mental scripts I'd internalized without consent. Every session gave me something—even if I didn't realize it at the time.

Over time, therapy became part of my rhythm. Like going to the gym or studying for the GMAT. You don't lift once and expect to be strong. You don't study once and expect an MBA. And you don't go to therapy once and expect lifelong emotional balance. It's reps. It's form. It's discipline.

These days, I still use therapy—but I also supplement with daily mental stretching. I use ChatGPT to reframe spirals, clarify thoughts, or build calm before conversations. It's not therapy. It's a maintenance tool. Like a protein shake or stretching before bed. The real work still happens in the harder sessions—the vulnerable ones.

But that work pays off. Not in status. Not in accolades. In something quieter. You spend on therapy so you can spend less on damage control. Less on apology tours. Less on sleepless nights and reactive decisions. That's emotional ROI.

And no—"retail therapy" doesn't count. That's a dopamine detour, not a solution. What you need isn't a receipt. It's a reset.

You invest in therapy not because you're broken, but because you want to stay intact. It's maintenance. It's mental hygiene. It's choosing alignment over chaos. If your employer offers sessions? Take them. It's one of the few moments in corporate life where the return is genuinely in your favor.

Giving – Investing in the World You Want to Live In

We don't talk about this enough, but giving is a form of spending.

It's not charity. It's not virtue signaling. It's a deliberate transfer of value—from you, to the world you want to live in. You spend your time, your attention, your knowledge, or your money… and the return might be invisible, but it's deeply felt.

The most powerful thing I did with my time for nearly a decade wasn't tied to work or income. From 2007 to 2015, I coached lacrosse at underperforming high schools. These weren't elite athletes. Most of these kids had never picked up a stick before. They didn't walk in with confidence—they walked in with doubt. But I showed up, week after week, season after season. And so did they.

Over time, I watched them grow—not just as players, but as people. I've seen those same kids become husbands, fathers, and leaders in their own communities. I didn't do that for recognition. I did it because someone once showed up for me. Showing up—consistently, without strings—is a kind of currency too.

Sometimes giving looks like pulling someone aside before they make a financial mistake. I remember talking with a cook who was thinking of going back to school. He told me he was considering the University of Phoenix. I sat him down, ran the numbers, and showed him how community college could give him a better education for a fraction of the debt. He was already deep in a hole from for-profit education. I wasn't trying to be a hero. I just didn't want to watch him dig deeper without someone handing him a better shovel.

That's spending, too. Time. Knowledge. Presence. All freely given—because someone needed it.

But giving isn't just dollars. It's hours. It's showing up when it would be easier not to.

At Cox, I volunteered at dozens of community events—many tied to the company, but not just because it was expected. I showed up because I wanted to understand the city I lived in. I worked food bank shifts, joined back-to-school drives, sat in spaces that introduced me to the real struggles happening across San Diego. It wasn't about feeling good—it was about getting closer to the people who rarely get a seat at the table. That time taught me how deep the gaps really go—and how easy it is to ignore them when you're not looking.

That's not free time. That's a real cost. I paid it gladly—because the return was perspective, empathy, and a deeper sense of purpose than anything I got from just writing a check.

And then there's mentorship. I've mentored colleagues at Cox—especially women—who were navigating how to grow into leadership roles. I've worked with student-athletes trying to figure out how their skills translated beyond the field. It's never just about advice. Mentorship takes time. It takes care. You spend emotional energy holding space for someone else's growth, while they figure out who they are.

You don't always see the results right away. Sometimes you never do. But when you do... when you watch someone level up because you believed in them first? That's ROI you feel in your chest.

There are organizations doing this kind of work every day. Just in Time for Foster Youth is one of them—offering mentorship, resources, and stability for young adults aging out of the foster system. They don't just write checks. They build relationships. That's the kind of giving that changes lives—and it starts with someone willing to give their time, not just their wallet.

I give financially as well. Not millions, but enough to feel it. I support organizations like the San Diego Humane Society, Feeding San Diego, and Voice of San Diego. Not because I want a plaque on the wall—but because I want to live in a city where animals are protected, people don't go hungry, and the media still holds power to account.

Giving isn't always easy. Sometimes I skip something for myself to make space for it. But that's the point. It's spending aligned with the world I'm trying to build. I'm not waiting until I "make it." I'm spending now, in proportion to what I have—and trusting that when I need help, someone else will be doing the same.

Because government programs matter. I believe in them. But they don't catch everything. They don't see your neighbor who just lost their job or the single mom down the hall who's too proud to ask for help. That's where nonprofits, communities, and quiet helpers step in. That's where the best returns happen —not in your bank account, but in the bonds you strengthen.

Giving is spending. And sometimes, it's the wisest spend you'll ever make.

The Cost of a Good Life

You're spending something every day—whether it's money, time, energy, or care. That's the hidden math of life. It's not just about what's in your bank account. It's about what you give your hours to. What you hold space for. What you let matter.

If you're not paying attention, you might spend years numbing, grinding, pleasing, and coping... and wonder why you feel bankrupt at the end of it.

None of this is free. Time, therapy, giving—they all ask something from you. But smart spending now can spare you a heavier cost later. Put in the work early, and you may not have to dig out of the same holes down the road. You invest in clarity so you don't pay in chaos. You invest in community so you don't face crisis alone. These choices may not feel urgent today —but they're how you reduce the emotional interest rate on your future.

Because needing less isn't about settling. It's about strength. When you invest your energy into healing, into helping, into being present—you spend less chasing. Less proving. Less running on empty.

Just like with money, the goal isn't perfection. It's alignment.

Spend on what matters. Invest in what lasts. And remember: some of your highest returns will come from the things no one else sees... but you'll feel them in every part of the life you build.

Chapter 19: Education... Again.

We've talked about education before—back in Chapter 8, when I laid out how the wrong degree can trap you in debt or leave you paying for prestige that never pays you back. But that was the cautionary tale. This time, I want to flip the lens. Because education isn't just a trap to avoid —it's also one of the most powerful levers you can pull if you treat it like a spending decision, not just a rite of passage.

The Real Price of Learning

Education isn't free. Even when it's "free."

Walking into a public library sounds like a no-cost way to learn, right? But it still costs something. Time. Energy. Bus fare. Focus. The choice to sit with a book instead of sitting on your couch. You don't just pay in money—you pay in effort. That's the hidden spend no one talks about.

I always think about that line from Good Will Hunting—you know the one:

"You dropped a hundred and fifty grand on an education you coulda got for a dollar fifty in late fees at the public library."

It's a great line. But even that version isn't truly free. Because showing up to learn, again and again, when no one's making you? That costs something. It always does.

That's the point. Education—real education—is a spending decision.
Not just a personal one. A financial one. A lifestyle one.
Because when you choose to keep learning, you're investing in something bigger than information. You're investing in options. You're creating future leverage. You're building the kind of mental wealth that doesn't just help you get a job—it helps you

leave one. Shift careers. Spot risk. Stay ready when the economy turns.

So no, this isn't a chapter about going back to school just to get a diploma. It's about how we spend our way toward independence. How we use time, effort, and attention to build something worth more than a résumé line. Something that lasts.

You're already learning, by the way. Every time you fix a leaky faucet with a YouTube video. Every time you follow a TikTok recipe or decode a spreadsheet at work. The question is—what would happen if you named it? Tracked it? Built on it?

What if education wasn't a throwback to your past—but a tool for your future?

Education Isn't Just for Kids—It's a Lifelong Lever

Education is one of the biggest purchases you'll ever make. But most people don't treat it that way. They treat it like a rite of passage. Or a personal dream. Or something they'll get to when life slows down. But like housing or healthcare, education is a spend category with long-term consequences.

Spend wisely, and it boosts your income, opens up new career lanes, and shrinks your future financial stress.
Spend poorly, and you're locked into debt, working longer hours for a piece of paper that never paid you back.

So let's treat education like what it really is: a financial lever. Sometimes the smartest move isn't to spend more—it's to spend better.

Take community college. In most places, it's practically free. That's not an exaggeration. Between local funding, state subsidies, and tax-backed tuition programs, many courses cost less than a single car payment. Some are entirely free. That's not just "affordable"—that's pre-paid. Your taxes already covered the bill. Even if you rent, you've been paying into the system.

That means not taking advantage of it is like skipping a meal you already bought.
Or walking past a tool you paid for and refusing to use it.

It's not just about the price—it's about the return. These aren't fluff classes. They're job skills: automotive tech, coding, early childhood development, accounting, culinary arts, healthcare certification. They're designed to help you earn more or pivot quickly—without burying you in student loans.

Compare that to the prestige trap. Plenty of four-year universities—and especially for-profit colleges—charge luxury prices for credentials with zero guarantee of a job. They'll tell you the brand name is worth it. But ask yourself: is the logo on your diploma going to pay your rent? Or are you paying $80,000 for a résumé line that might not move the needle?

That's not education. That's brand worship. It's a bad spend.

And look—I'm not throwing stones from the outside. I went to Syracuse. Private university. National brand. Big tuition bill. Today, four years of undergraduate tuition alone will run you about $65,000 per year—that's $260,000 before you even factor in housing, books, or food.

I don't regret it. But I also don't pretend it was the most efficient financial decision. At the time, it felt like momentum. Like the "right" path. But now? I see how much of that cost was branding. If I were advising someone else today—especially someone without a financial safety net—I'd say: spend differently. Not less, but smarter. Use public options. Reject prestige unless it comes with a return.

Because not all high-cost education is a bad spend—if the ROI is real.

My MBA from UCLA Anderson is proof of that. I attended their Fully Employed MBA program, which runs about $46,000 per year in tuition, or roughly $138,000 over three years.

Here's why that spend made sense:

- It's tax-deductible in many cases as a business expense, which immediately lowers the true cost.
- You can keep working while enrolled—so you're not losing income while you learn.
- And the ROI is massive: Anderson reports average post-MBA salary jumps of 60% or more. For many grads, that means going from $100K to $170K+ within a year or two. That's a $70,000 raise—more than half the entire cost of the degree.

That's not a hope. That's math.
It's exactly the kind of spend that builds financial power instead of draining it.

I wasn't just buying a diploma. I was buying leverage. And I knew exactly what I was paying for.

Where we should be demanding more value is in policy: making sure community college credits transfer to public universities without friction or extra fees. Right now, that's a money game. State schools don't always accept the credits because they want you in their system longer—paying more. That's not about quality. That's about profit. And we should be furious about it.

Because education should be a public good—and public goods should be structured for mobility, not monetization.

Beyond community college, there are non-predatory trade schools, certificate programs, and online academies that offer solid ROI. The key is to treat every option like a product:

- What does it cost?
- How long will it take to pay off?
- Will it earn you more money, more flexibility, or more leverage?

If the answer's yes, that's a spend worth considering.
If the answer's no? Walk away.

In this book, education isn't just framed as self-improvement—it's framed as spending strategy. And like every spend in your life, the smartest choice isn't the flashiest. It's the one that gives you the most back.

Education Costs More Than Money—It Costs Time

Education doesn't just cost money. It costs time.
And time, as we've already covered, is your most limited resource.

That's been one of the running themes of this book: you only get 24 hours a day. That's your true budget. When you choose to invest in learning—whether it's an online class, a podcast during your commute, or a certification course on weekends—you're not just spending time. You're spending your future hours differently.

Because every hour you spend building a skill today is an hour you won't have to spend panicking later. Or job hunting under pressure. Or working overtime just to keep up.

That's the trade-off.
You give up time now to buy back time later.

And I've lived that trade-off.

Just getting into my MBA program at UCLA Anderson took an enormous time investment. I studied for the GMAT like it was a second job—five hours a day, every weekday. I'd get to work by 6:00 a.m. just so I could study from 6:00 to 8:00. I squeezed in another hour during lunch, and then another 90 minutes from 5:00 to 6:30 before heading out to coach lacrosse. That was my life. For months. No shortcuts, no guarantees.

And that was just to get in.

Once I started the program, the time cost only grew. For three years, I gave my nights and weekends to learning. I did homework after work. I spent evenings buried in group projects. Every Saturday, from 9:30 to 5:15, I was in class. It was non-stop. I put friendships on pause. I didn't really have time to date. I missed weddings. I skipped events. I said no to a lot of "fun" things—not because I didn't want to go, but because I had made a different kind of commitment.

That was the cost. At times, it felt like a lot.
But that sacrifice? It changed my earning power. It sharpened how I think. It created openings I never would have had otherwise. Today, I can say with confidence: it was worth every hour.

Not because the classes were perfect or the workload was easy —but because I spent my time with intention. I treated it like a resource. Like a currency. Like something I could use to build something bigger.

And the return isn't always fast. Not every class pays off immediately. Not every credential gets noticed on a résumé. But like compound interest, the investment stacks. Quietly. Gradually. Until one day, someone asks a question—and you know the answer. A door opens—and you're qualified to walk through it. You're not guessing anymore. You're ready.

That's the ROI most people never calculate. They see the hours they lose, not the dollars they protect. But education is one of the few ways you can spend time now to reduce how much life costs you later.

It's the long game.
And yeah, it's a grind. You won't always feel smart in the moment. Some days, it'll feel like a waste. But over time, it builds. Knowledge grows. Confidence compounds. One day, you realize—you're no longer trying to catch up. You're ahead. Now, I get it—not everyone has the same runway I had. You might have kids. A partner. A sick parent. A second job. Your time budget might already feel maxed out. You're not ignoring growth—you're just busy surviving.

But that's why it's even more important to be strategic. You don't need to upend your life to start learning. You just need to start small.

Education isn't passive. It's one of the most active ways you can spend your time. And the best part? You get to choose the currency.

- Watch a 20-minute YouTube tutorial
- Listen to a podcast during your walk
- Audit a free course
- Block one hour a week for learning, just like you'd block it for a workout

Because you don't need to go back to school to get smarter. But you do need to spend your time like it matters. Because it does.

Unlike money, time never refunds.

Don't Overlook What You've Already Paid For

If I told you there was $5,000 sitting in a drawer in your house, you'd tear the place apart to find it.
But when that $5,000 shows up as unused education benefits you've already helped fund—through your taxes, your labor, or your paycheck deductions—most people never go looking.

That's the gap we're closing right now.

Because when it comes to education, you've already paid for more than you think.
Through taxes. Through your employer. Through your time spent showing up for a job you're trying to get better at. And too many people leave those benefits on the table.

Let's start with one of the biggest: employer-sponsored education.

A lot of companies offer tuition reimbursement—sometimes up to $5,250 a year—for classes, certifications, or degree programs. That's a free check with your name on it. But most employees never claim it, either because they don't know it exists or they assume it's only for senior managers. It's not.

Check your HR portal. Look in the benefits section of your onboarding materials. Ask your manager. Sometimes, the program is so underused that you'll be the first person in years to even bring it up. That's not a bad thing—it makes you look ambitious and proactive.

Even if your company doesn't offer formal tuition support, they might still be open to helping—if you make the case.

That's one of the simplest MBA lessons out there: most people don't say no—they just wait for someone to ask.

If a class, certificate, or degree would directly make you better at your job, pitch it.

Explain the return: how it'll improve your performance, help your team, or allow you to take on more responsibility. Companies want people who are leveling up. Show them that supporting your growth is a smart investment—not a favor.

Even if they won't pay for tuition outright, they might:

- Cover the cost of materials
- Approve learning time during slow cycles
- Let you expense a course or conference
- Create a stretch project aligned with your new skillset

The bottom line? If you don't ask, the answer is already no. If you do ask—especially with a clear ROI—they might say yes.

Don't stop at work. Local governments offer community education programs, vocational training, GED prep, citizenship classes, and continuing education—many of which are already funded with your taxes. This is Principle #5 in action: your government can make your life easier, but only if you demand and use what you've already paid for. Leaving those resources untouched is like handing money back to the same system that too often favors billionaires over everyday people.

And it's not just government. Community counts too. When you join a co-op childcare swap, share transportation, or lean on a free tutoring group at the library, you're participating in a safety net that's older than any policy: each other. It only works if you show up for others when they need you, too.

So the smartest spend isn't always new. Sometimes it's reclaiming what you've already bought—through your paycheck, through your taxes, through your relationships.

If you're trying to recession-proof your life, climb the ladder, or just shift directions without adding more financial weight—start here. Audit your access.

- What benefits has your company already promised you?
- What programs have your taxes already paid for in your city or county?
- What resources are bundled into subscriptions or insurance you're already funding?

You don't need to be overwhelmed by options—you need to be informed about opportunities you've already earned.
Reclaim what's yours. Don't just use it—leverage it. You've already paid for the tools. Now use them to build not just your future, but a stronger one for the people around you too.

Start With a Plan, Even if the Plan Changes

If education is a spend—and it is—then you need a plan for how you're spending it.
Not just a hope. Not just a vague intention. A real plan. Even if that plan changes later.

Because smart spending is never aimless. You don't throw money at random. You allocate it based on what you need, what you're building toward, and what you can afford. Learning should work the same way.

Ask yourself:

- What's my end goal?
- Will this help me earn more, think better, or contribute differently?
- Is this the best use of my time and money right now?

I know what it's like to have the plan change.

x

When I applied to business school, I wasn't planning on doing it part-time. My original goal was to enroll in a two-year, full-time MBA program, leave work behind, and transition into consulting. That was the plan. That was the timeline. That was the spend I expected—both financially and personally.

But things shifted.
I got bumped into the part-time program. Everything changed with it.

My approach had to shift. My time became a premium. My relationships changed. I couldn't just go to every networking event or relocate for a summer internship. I had to stay working full-time while studying. The spend shifted from tuition-only to a constant daily tradeoff between work, school, sleep, and the people in my life.

I didn't get the education experience I originally imagined—but I got one that forced me to be more deliberate with every single dollar and every single hour.

And you know what? It worked out. Not because it was easy. But because I adapted. I adjusted my plan without abandoning the goal. I kept moving forward.

That's what I mean when I say: start with a plan, even if the plan changes.
Because life will disrupt your original script. And your success won't come from how perfectly you follow that script—it'll come from how well you pivot when things shift under your feet.

If you're just starting out—or coming straight from high school —exploration is part of the plan. That's okay. Try different subjects. Sample classes. Learn what you like and what you hate. That's still forward motion.

But if you're already working, raising kids, or trying to shift careers, your learning plan needs more focus. You don't have unlimited time. You don't have the luxury of throwing money at vague ideas. You need intentional learning—the kind that builds income, freedom, or stability.

Because here's the real power move: the right education doesn't just help you make more money. It can help you need less of it. That's Principle #4—needing less is power. If you can earn the same income in fewer hours, or shift to a job with benefits that save you money elsewhere (healthcare, flexibility, retirement), your whole financial life starts to bend in your favor.

So don't just ask, "Will this program get me promoted?"
Ask, "Will this let me work fewer hours without losing income?"
Or, "Will this give me more control over how I spend my days?"

That's ROI. That's smart spending.

Remember: degrees and certificates aren't magic. They're paper. What they really show is effort. A willingness to commit. To organize your thinking. To learn a set of tools and apply them in the field.

That application part? That's what separates a résumé line from a real skill.

The best education doesn't just teach you what to think. It teaches you how to think. It sharpens judgment. It builds pattern recognition. It helps you see what others miss.

That's why internships, apprenticeships, and project work are still some of the most underrated forms of education out there. If you're young and reading this—get your foot in the door somewhere. Anything. If you're older? Find a stretch project at your current job that forces you to learn something new. Both routes work the same muscle.

Because real growth happens when you learn something… and then use it.

Learning Isn't Just Personal—It's Communal

We talk about education like it's an individual journey.
Your goals. Your investment. Your ROI. Your life.

But that's only part of the story.

Because every time you choose to learn something new, you're not just spending for yourself—you're raising the baseline for everyone around you.

When you pursue learning with intention, you model it. You normalize it. You make it easier for the next person to follow your path.

Your coworkers notice. Your family notices. Your kids—if you have them—absorb it. Your community quietly shifts. Even if no one says anything, your commitment becomes a signal: we're allowed to grow here.

Especially in communities where college wasn't the norm, where confidence was systemically stripped, or where education was framed as something for "other people"—your learning becomes a form of resistance. Of restoration.

This is where spending gets communal too.
Because when public education is underused, it gets underfunded.
When tuition reimbursement programs go unclaimed, companies quietly cut them.
When we fail to advocate for learning that fits real lives— affordable, flexible, meaningful—those options disappear.

That's Principle #4 in action: needing less becomes power— especially when it allows you to reinvest in others.

Principle #5: your government can help—but only if you demand it.

Because being the first person in your circle to sign up for a course?
Or finish a degree?
Or learn a trade and teach it to someone else?

That's a spend with ripple effects.
It shows up in financial decisions, parenting choices, local leadership, and peer mentorship. It spreads.

Smart learning is contagious.

So no—this chapter wasn't just about education.
It was about strategy. About awareness. About community return.

You don't need to do everything. But you do need to start. Because learning isn't just about self-improvement. It's a form of collective investment.

What's the return on that?

Exponential.

The Real Return

Education isn't a one-time event. It's a direction you can keep steering toward, even if you took the long way around.

If you know where you're going, learning is the fuel. If you don't, learning is the map.

Too many people treat education like a locked gate—something they passed through once and left behind. But it was never a gate. It was a launchpad. A tool belt. A gym membership for your brain. And just like your body, your mind atrophies when you stop using it.

You don't need to go back to school to get smarter.
But you do need to get deliberate.
Watch a lecture. Take a free class. Ask your HR rep about tuition aid. Hell, just ask a friend what they're reading and start there. Because the truth is: we all learn best when we're curious—and we retain the most when we apply it.

And more than anything?
Learning is a way of spending your time wisely.
It's not just about what you pay.
It's about how you invest your days.
Education, when used intentionally, is not a debt—it's a dividend.
It pays out in better jobs, stronger communities, smarter conversations, and deeper self-worth. Most of the time? It's already paid for.
Use it. Stack it. Share it. Shape it into something that works for you… and for everyone you might lift up along the way.

Once you realize how much you've already learned…
You start to see just how much you still can.

Because the smartest people in the room aren't always the loudest.
They're the ones who never stopped asking questions.

Chapter 20: The Financial Fire Drill

There's a moment after every major crisis—when the dust settles, the adrenaline fades, and you're left with the question: "Now what?"

Some people freeze. Others crumble. But a few? They move with clarity. Not because they're stronger. Not because they're fearless. But because they were ready.

I've come to believe that the break is inevitable. The response is everything.

That's how I view financial crisis, too. Not as something to fear —or even something you can always prevent—but something you can prepare for.

The earthquake is coming. The layoff. The diagnosis. The accident. The phone call that shifts your entire life sideways. The world doesn't wait until you're ready to fall apart. It just… does.

When it does, even if everything else stops… the bills won't. That's the brutal math of a crisis: money keeps moving whether you're ready or not.

That's why this chapter exists. Not to scare you—but to build your emergency plan. Your financial go-bag. Your 30-day lifeboat.

Because the moment you hit the floor, your survival depends not on how smart you are—but on how clearly you've already defined what matters most.

And that's where spending becomes more than a budget. It becomes your lifeline.

I've lived in San Diego since 2006, and I still remember the 1994 Northridge earthquake like it was yesterday. Not because I felt it—San Diego was spared—but because I saw the aftermath on the news: highways split open, buildings pancaked, entire communities reduced to rubble. From that moment on, I kept a packed emergency bag. Just in case.

Food. Water. Batteries. A flashlight. Medications. A few basic clothes. That bag made me feel like I could survive a worst-case scenario. While it wasn't pretty, it meant that if the Big One ever hit, I wouldn't be completely helpless.

But here's the twist: most people never pack one for their money.

They go into financial crisis with no plan, no budget, no idea what they actually need to survive the next 30 days. They're caught off guard not just by the emergency itself, but by how fast their spending becomes unsustainable. Rent is still due. Groceries still cost money. The gas tank doesn't refill itself. When you're already reeling emotionally, the last thing you want is to make 50 financial decisions from scratch.
So in this chapter, we build your financial go-bag.

We figure out what matters most, what can be cut, and what your minimum cost of survival actually is. We start with a 30-day lifeboat—the financial version of a three-day earthquake kit —and we build from there. Because when the shock comes, and it will, the person you become after will depend a lot on the plan you made before.

A Reminder: This Isn't the First Time Power Got This Lopsided.

The last time wealth piled this high and wages stayed this flat, it was the Gilded Age—an era of extreme opulence for the few, and quiet suffering for everyone else.

It took decades to claw our way out.

Not just through income taxes and regulation, but through a
new understanding: that society collapses when too much
money concentrates at the top.

You don't need to be a historian to see the rhyme.
We're living in a modern version of it now—one wrapped in
stock buybacks and crypto hype instead of railroads and steel.
But the problem is the same: a system too rigged to function for
the average person, and too polite to name who broke it.

That's why your financial philosophy isn't just personal—it's
political.
When you understand the system, you start asking better
questions.
Not "How do I get rich?"
But "Why do the rules work so well for people who already are?

We clawed our way out of the last Gilded Age by demanding
more—not just from ourselves, but from the systems meant to
protect us. That option still exists… if we push for it.

Your 30-Day Lifeboat Budget

If I asked you right now, "What does it cost you to survive for
30 days?"—could you answer with confidence? Not thrive. Not
coast. Not catch up on debts or buy a single luxury. Just survive.
Shelter, food, water, basic utilities, medicine, and the most
essential form of transportation. Could you tell me the number?

Most people can't.

That's not a criticism. It's a reflection of how few of us are
taught to build our budgets from the ground up. We're taught
to aspire, to dream, to calculate raises and retirement—but
rarely are we taught how to tread water financially when life
pulls us under. That's what a lifeboat budget is for.

A lifeboat budget isn't elegant. It isn't something you'd show off on social media. But it's the first step in making sure that when life breaks down, you don't. Because in a true crisis, your goal isn't to maintain your lifestyle. It's to stay afloat.

So let's break it down.

What About Your Automated Savings?

If you've been following along since earlier chapters, you might already have part of your paycheck automatically sweeping into savings or investments before you ever see it. That's one of the best financial habits you can build.

But in a true 30-day crisis, even the best habits sometimes need to flex.

For now, don't panic and cancel those transfers. First, run your lifeboat budget. Figure out the bare minimum you need to stay afloat. If your automated savings or investment contributions make it impossible to hit that survival number, it's okay to pause them temporarily.

This isn't failure. This is triage.

The moment the storm passes—whether it's a layoff ending, medical bills slowing down, or a new job starting—turn that automation back on. Even if it's a smaller amount than before, restarting that habit is what keeps a short-term crisis from turning into long-term instability.

Remember: automation isn't about perfection. It's about consistency over time. Pausing when you're drowning doesn't erase your progress. It just buys you oxygen so you can swim again.

Step One: Define Your Essentials

This is the moment you strip your budget to the studs. What do you absolutely need in order to survive 30 days? Not what makes you comfortable. Not what helps you unwind. Just what keeps you upright.

Here's a basic framework:

- Shelter – Rent or mortgage. No exceptions. This is non-negotiable. You lose this, the rest crumbles.
- Food – Bare-bones grocery list. Staples like rice, beans, oats, eggs, frozen veggies, canned goods. Not takeout. Not organic-only. Just enough to get through.
- Utilities – Power, water, and basic internet if needed for work. Cut premium cable, extra streaming, home security subscriptions, and anything that doesn't directly support daily function.
- Transportation – If you need a car to work or care for others, keep gas in the tank. If public transit is an option, switch. Cancel car washes, ride shares, or long-distance commutes unless essential.
- Medical – Prescriptions, insurance premiums, or out-of-pocket care. This stays.

Now add those up. Not roughly. Not in your head. Write it down.

You're building your 30-day number—the one you need to remember like your own birthday.

The clearer that number becomes, the more you realize how little it actually takes to survive. That's not scarcity—it's strength.

Step Two: Audit the Non-Essentials

This is where it gets uncomfortable. You start confronting where your money has been going out of habit instead of need.

Subscriptions? Gone.
Gym membership? Pause it.
Alcohol, lattes, dinners out? Save the treat for when the storm passes.

You don't cut these because they're morally wrong. You cut them because they don't keep you alive. That's the line. If it's not helping you survive the next 30 days, it goes. Even if it's fun. Even if it's your coping mechanism. Even if it's been in your budget for years.

This part isn't about shame—it's about preservation.

Step Three: Find Your Floor

Let's say your normal spending is $3,400/month. After cutting aggressively, you discover you can survive on $1,750 if you really had to.

That $1,750? That's your floor. That's your financial oxygen mask.

Once you have that number, you stop feeling like you're falling with no parachute. Now you know: if everything goes wrong, this is what I need to get through the next 30 days. Not more. Not less.

Real World Example: The Math of It All

Let's say this is your actual lifeboat budget:

30-Day Lifeboat Budget

Category	Monthly Cost
Rent	$1,200
Groceries	$200
Utilities	$100
Transportation	$100
Medical	$150
Total	**$1,750**

Now compare that to your current income—or unemployment benefits, or side hustle potential. Can you cover it? If not, you know exactly how short you'll fall—and how much support you'll need to bridge the gap.

If you can cover it, every extra dollar becomes oxygen. It gives you time to breathe, reassess, and re-stabilize. It buys you options.

When Awareness Feels Like Failure

There's something quietly powerful about having that number in your back pocket. It doesn't mean life won't shake you. But it does mean you'll shake less. Because the second you go into crisis mode—whatever the trigger—you won't be scrambling. You'll already know where to go, what to cut, and how to focus your energy.

When you know your number, you protect your brain from spiraling.

You save your emotional bandwidth for the call you need to make, the résumé you need to update, the doctor you need to see. You're not wasting calories trying to reinvent your finances mid-storm.

This isn't how you want to live, but it's how you survive.

Your lifeboat budget isn't your forever plan. It's not something to live in for months at a time. It's a fallback, a floor, a reminder that even when everything else is falling apart—you don't have to.
Once you know your number, you can build the next layer of protection on top of it.

That's what we'll do next.

Cut Fast, Cut Smart

In a financial crisis, the most dangerous thing you can do is hesitate.

The clock doesn't pause while you figure things out. Bills are still coming. Interest is still ticking. Your body still needs food. Your rent, your car, your child's lunch—none of them care that you're "working on a plan."

That's why you can't wait for permission to act. You have to cut fast—and you have to cut smart.

This isn't a reckless slash. It's not about panicking and canceling everything in a flurry of anxiety. It's the opposite. It's methodical. It's surgical. You're not destroying your lifestyle— you're preserving your financial life.

The goal here is simple: protect your active spending power when everything else starts to slip.

Build a Crisis Cut List

Think of your spending like a traffic light system. You need clarity fast, and color-coded clarity works. You don't need a spreadsheet. You need a gut-check system that tells you where the knife goes first.

RED – Cut Immediately

These are the expenses that provide little-to-no value in a crisis:

- Subscription boxes (clothing, snacks, wine, etc.)
- Most streaming services (you can keep one at most)
- Delivery apps and convenience fees
- Gym memberships if you can work out at home
- Any automated donations, club memberships, or services you can pause

These are your financial leaks. In normal times, they're fine. In survival mode, they're indulgent liabilities.

If it's not helping you stay housed, fed, or healthy, it needs to go on Day 1.

YELLOW – Evaluate and Adjust

These are case-by-case. You don't cut them blindly, but you do put them on the chopping block if they don't serve your new reality.

- Grocery spending (downgrade to basics, frozen foods, generics)
- Car costs (can you take public transit or drive less?)
- Phone plans (can you downgrade to a basic plan or ask for temporary assistance?)
- Internet (can you reduce speed temporarily or cancel extras?)

This tier is where most people get stuck. They think, "Well, I kind of need this…" Maybe. But in a real emergency, even these "essentials" are flexible.

The real question is: Can I reduce this without breaking something critical?

GREEN – Protect at All Costs

These are your lifelines. Touch them last.

- Rent/mortgage
- Health insurance and prescriptions
- Utility minimums (especially power and water)
- Transportation to work or essential caregiving
- Childcare or school-related costs (if they keep your family afloat)

These are your non-negotiables. Without these, the whole system collapses. You protect them by cutting everything else before you ever let them lapse.

The Emotional Cost of Cutting

Let's not pretend this is easy.

A crisis cut list sounds rational on paper. But in real life, it means confronting the reality that your lifestyle might shrink for a while. It means canceling things that brought you comfort, convenience, or status.

You'll feel it. You'll wonder if it makes you look broke. You'll get emails reminding you "Your subscription is about to end!" and it'll sting—because everything around us is designed to make us feel like cutting back is a failure.

But it's not.

Cutting smart is an act of control. It's a refusal to spiral. It's a way of saying, "I may be hurting right now, but I'm still in charge of how my money moves."

The truth is, the faster you cut, the less permanent the damage becomes. Every dollar you don't spend now is a dollar that buys you time to recover.

Pre-Crisis Planning: Make the List Now

Here's the real power move: build your cut list before you're in crisis.

Sit down on a calm day. Go through your bank statements. Color-code your expenses—red, yellow, green. Then save that list somewhere you can find it fast.

This isn't paranoia. It's preparedness.

In a storm, the worst thing you can do is freeze. If your brain already knows what to do—if the plan is written, clear, and accessible—you don't lose precious time figuring it out under pressure.

You just execute.

That's the difference between people who float through a crisis and those who sink.

Short term pain, long term sanity:

The cut isn't punishment. It's preservation. You're not taking away your lifestyle. You're protecting the life you're still going to build.

The Emotional Cost of Knowing Your Number

At first, knowing your survival number feels like power. You finally see the baseline. You know what it costs to stay upright. That clarity is rare.

But then comes the grief. Because once you know that number, you can't unsee how much of your past spending was noise. You start to feel the weight of it—the fragility, the habits, the blind spots. It stings.

Here's where many people spiral. They think, "How did I let it get this bad?" or "Why didn't I save more?" But pause that.

You didn't fail. You just finally looked.

The truth is, you were never meant to. The system is designed to keep you distracted—auto-pay, lifestyle creep, subscriptions that lull you into spending while you're asleep.

Nobody taught you how to build a lifeboat. So how could you feel guilty for never having one?

Now that you've built it, you're ahead of most people. Once you've looked directly at your worst-case scenario, everything else starts to look a little less scary.

The Shift in Perspective

Knowing your number doesn't just affect your budget. It affects your identity.

You start to think in survival terms. Not in a paranoid way—but in a practical, almost military way. You begin measuring your days in cost per hour. You recognize which purchases feel like indulgences and which feel like anchors. You begin seeing every dollar not just as money, but as time.

It doesn't make you stingy. It makes you strategic.

That $70 dinner you used to grab on impulse? That's half your grocery budget in crisis mode.
The streaming bundle you haven't touched in weeks? That's gas to get to an interview.
The morning coffee and muffin? That's three days of ramen if you lose your job.

These realizations don't make you weak. They make you sharper.

Once you've felt that sharpness—once you've run your hands over the edges of your real costs—you can't un-feel it.

What to Do With the Emotion

Don't shove the emotion away. Use it.

If you're angry? Good. Let it fuel your next steps.

If you're scared? Write that down. Track the fear to its source—then create a plan to reduce it, step by step.

If you feel ashamed or small or behind? Name it. But don't let it define your next decision. You are not the mistake. You are the person fixing it.

And this is where money turns back into movement.

This is where knowing your number isn't just about crisis—it's about clarity. It's about knowing how to build back when life gives you the chance.

Don't Overcorrect the Mistake

When you're driving and realize you've missed your exit, the worst thing you can do is panic and yank the wheel. That's how accidents happen. The smarter move? Keep calm, take the next exit, and reroute.

Financial mistakes work the same way.

You bought something you regret. You overspent on vacation. You didn't track your spending for a month. Okay. But don't spiral into panic mode. Don't empty your savings or punish yourself with a "no-spend" month that makes life miserable.

Pause. Breathe. Backtrack when you're ready. The worst financial crashes come from people trying too hard to undo a mistake all at once—cutting things too quickly, skipping bills, or selling investments at a loss just to "fix it."

You're allowed to course-correct slowly. Missing one exit doesn't mean you never reach your destination. It just means you're human.

Because once you've looked directly at your worst-case scenario, everything else starts to look a little less scary. You've seen the floor. You know it didn't break you.

You've felt the fear. You've mapped the floor. And now you know—needing less isn't weakness. It's your new advantage.

Knowledge is emotional clarity:

Knowing your number doesn't make you fragile. It makes you fluent.
Fluency in crisis—that's the beginning of real resilience.

That's exactly where we go next—taking that resilience and baking it into every dollar you spend going forward.

Chapter 21: The Resilience Reserve

L et's say you made it through the storm. You used your lifeboat budget. You cut fast, cut smart. You leaned on your village when you had to. It wasn't graceful—but it worked. You're upright. Maybe a little battered, maybe still behind, but breathing. That alone is a win.

So now the question becomes: What do you do with that experience?

You build a resilience reserve.

This isn't just an emergency fund—although yes, it starts there. This is something deeper. It's a financial habit built from emotional clarity. It's the decision to create distance between you and the next crisis.

It begins with something small: $10 a day.

Start With the Psychology, Not the Math

Ten bucks a day doesn't sound like much. But that's the point. You're not trying to save thousands all at once. You're trying to retrain your instincts.

You're shifting a tiny slice of your active spend into your passive protection plan.

It's the coffee you didn't buy.
The Lyft you didn't take.
The shirt you didn't need.
The app you canceled.
The second drink you passed on.

All that money wasn't gone. It was just hiding. Every day, you're already spending it—you're just not spending it on your future.

So here's what happens when you redirect it:

- $10/day = $300/month
- $300/month = $3,600/year
- In 5 years, that's $18,000—before interest.
- Add in some investment returns, and you're flirting with $20K.

In other words... your crisis buffer.

Why $20K is the New Emergency Target

Some people still say $1,000 is enough for an emergency. Others say three months of expenses. Then six.
But in today's economy? That bar is too low.

After everything we've lived through—layoffs, rent hikes, $5,000 car repairs, $6,000 ER visits—$20,000 isn't excessive. It's realistic.

You're not saving for a rainy day anymore. You're saving for the storm you already lived through.

Then it was three months of expenses.

Then six.

But post-2020? In a world of layoffs, hospital bills, rent hikes, and rising food costs—$20,000 is no longer excessive. It's reasonable.

Here's why:

- One major car repair can run $4,000.
- A single ER visit can be $6,000+ without insurance.
- Moving across the country for work? Easily $5,000–$8,000.
- Job hunting for 6 months while paying rent? That's your entire fund.

The goal isn't to reach $20K tomorrow. The goal is to treat it like your true north. A compass point you walk toward, day by day, without losing sight of why it matters.

This is the money that makes decisions easier. It lets you quit a toxic job. Move out of an unhealthy situation. Say yes to an opportunity across the country. Sleep at night when the layoff rumors start.

It's not a luxury. It's the foundation.

Where the Money Comes From: Active vs. Passive Revisited

Remember our earlier framing: Passive spending is what happens without effort. Active spending is what you choose.

The key to building your resilience reserve is converting passive leaks into intentional deposits.

Here's what that looks like in action:

- Cancel a $25/month app? Redirect that $25 to savings.
- Eat out two times less this month? That's $60 in your reserve.
- Cut one impulse Amazon order? Another $40 preserved.

You don't need to overhaul your life. You just need to track what used to slip away unnoticed—and give it a new destination.

This is the quiet engine of your reserve. You won't feel it working at first. But months from now, when you open that account and see four figures staring back at you, you'll know: this isn't hypothetical anymore. This is safety, built choice by choice.

Automate It Like a Bill

The best way to protect your reserve from yourself? Treat it like rent.

Pick a daily or weekly amount—$10/day or $70/week.
Set an automatic transfer.
Make it non-negotiable.
Make it invisible.

This isn't savings that gets raided for concert tickets. This isn't your travel fund. This isn't the "I've been good, I deserve this" account.

This is future-you's lifeline. Untouchable. Sacred.

If you want to spend more money on your present self, fine—go earn it. But don't rob your future self to buy takeout.

Give It a Name

Psychologists have proven that we respect accounts more when we personalize them. So don't just call it "savings." That's abstract.

Call it:

- The Lifeboat Fund
- The Reset Account
- The Walk-Away Money
- The F***-It Fund (if you're feeling spicy)
- The Stay-Standing Fund

Whatever feels real to you.

Because one day, that name will feel like hope.

You don't know the what, but you do know how to react

The resilience reserve isn't built on fear. It's built on freedom.

It's not about bracing for the worst—it's about giving yourself options when life shifts underneath you. The money you're setting aside isn't just a buffer. It's a boundary. It lets you step back, catch your breath, and choose what happens next without panic holding the pen.

Because when the next disruption hits—and it will—this is the money that says:
"You don't owe anyone your suffering this time."

You can walk away from the job.
Pause the chaos.
Take the time.
Say no.
Say yes.
Stand still.

This isn't a savings account. It's your soft landing.

Once you know it's there…
You stop living like everything depends on the next paycheck.

You start spending like your life has structure.
You start living like your time is your own.

Because it is.

Now you're ready to use it on purpose.

Chapter 22: Spending for the Life You Want

There's this lie we've all been sold: that financial stability is something you achieve alone. That if you just work hard enough, save diligently enough, plan perfectly enough—you'll never have to rely on anyone.

That's fantasy.

The truth is, we all need people. Especially in crisis. Especially when the numbers don't work. Especially when the emotional math is too heavy to carry on your own.

If we're going to talk about spending—as in real spending, the kind that buys time, hope, mobility—then we have to talk about how people show up in your budget. Because sometimes, the most strategic financial decision you can make is to ask for help before swiping a card.

That help comes at a cost—but not the kind you expect. It might cost a little ego. A little pride. A little vulnerability. But it can save you thousands of dollars, months of recovery, or years of debt.

Help Is a Form of Currency

Sometimes your best financial move isn't cutting costs. It's calling someone.

That could mean:

- Asking a sibling if you can crash for two months while job hunting
- Calling a friend to borrow their car for a week
- Accepting a grocery drop-off instead of pretending you're fine
- Telling your boss you need two extra days before rent hits

These aren't moments of weakness. These are flashes of strategy. Because the alternative? It's not just financially worse—it's emotionally costlier.

We romanticize doing it alone, but let's do the actual math:

- Two months of rent in a crisis = $3,200
- Interest from putting it on a credit card = $700 over time
- Borrowing a room and making dinner once a week in return = maybe $200

That's a $3,700 swing.
And yet we hesitate—because we think asking for help is admitting failure.
But asking for help before you're desperate? That's not weakness. That's risk management.

It's also a form of active spending.
Not in dollars—but in dignity, conversation, and trust. You're choosing how to spend your emotional and social currency. Just like financial capital, emotional capital needs to be invested wisely.

Build the Village Before You Need It

Strong communities don't build themselves. They're made in the cracks—when someone remembers your birthday, checks in after a layoff, or shows up with soup when you're sick.

So if you want to build a financial life that doesn't collapse the moment something goes wrong, you have to treat people like part of the plan.

Not a backup. A pillar.

Investing in your social safety net means:

- Hosting dinner when you can afford it
- Lending an ear even when you're tired
- Sending a "thinking of you" message without needing anything back
- Showing up for others before the storm comes

Here's what no bank account can do: pick up your kid when you're stuck in traffic, give you a reference when you're laid off, or sit with you when your plans fall apart.

The best financial strategy for hard times might be this:
Be the kind of person people are glad they said yes to.

And that starts long before you need the favor.

Ask With Clarity, Not Shame

Here's how you ask for help without guilt:
You treat it like any other resource decision. Not an act of desperation... an act of optimization.

You wouldn't feel ashamed asking for a lower interest rate.
You wouldn't feel guilty comparing phone plans.
So why treat people differently?

The key is intentionality.

Here's the real framework:

1. **Be clear about the ask**
   - "Can I borrow $200 to get through this week?"
   - "Can I crash on your couch for 14 days while I reset?"
   - "Can you help with rides this month while I figure out transportation?"

2. **Set the container**
   - Define a time frame.
   - Define what success looks like.
   - Define what you'll do in return, even if it's non-financial.

3. **Be emotionally honest**
   - Don't pretend you're fine.
   - But don't collapse in the process either.
   - You're not a burden—you're a person in transition.

4. **Show the plan**
   - People support progress.
   - "Here's what I'm doing to get back on track" is more compelling than "Please help me."
   - You don't need perfection—just movement.

When you bring structure to the ask, you reduce the emotional cost for both of you.

It becomes less about charity, and more about partnership in hard times.

You are not begging.

You are leveraging a human resource—the same way you would leverage a tool, a job lead, or a 0% balance transfer.

In the long run, the relationships that survive these asks are the ones worth protecting.

Help Without Harming Each Other

There's a line between support and sacrifice—and it's thinner than we like to admit.

When someone you care about is in crisis, your first instinct might be to overextend.
To say yes before you think.
To swipe the card, write the check, move mountains…

But if the help bankrupts you emotionally or financially, it's not help.
It's a transfer of instability.

Real support doesn't just solve their problem—it preserves your foundation, too.

Here's how to help wisely:

1. **Be honest about your limits**
   - "I can't lend $500, but I can do $100."
   - "I can't house you indefinitely, but I can give you a week."
   - "I can't loan money, but I can help you apply for aid or update your résumé."

2. **Offer alternatives instead of apologies**
   - Emotional support is real support.
   - Time, logistics, or connections are often more valuable than money.
   - Don't assume financial help is the only meaningful kind.

3. **Frame your help like a budget**
   - Set a cap.
   - Make the terms clear.
   - Protect your other obligations—your rent, your bills, your own emergency fund.

4. **Say no without guilt**
   - Saying no doesn't mean you stopped caring.
   - It means you're aware that two drowning people don't make a rescue.
   - You're not a villain for protecting your own oxygen mask.

Boundaries make your support sustainable.
They ensure that your act of care doesn't turn into quiet resentment down the line.
If someone reacts poorly to your boundaries, that's not a crisis—it's clarity.

Mutual Aid Is the Original Insurance

Before we had credit scores and overdraft protection...
before banks sold overdraft lines and payday lenders waited on corners...
before GoFundMe became the emergency safety net for millions...

We had each other.

Mutual aid isn't a new idea. It's the oldest form of financial resilience.

- Neighbors shared groceries when someone lost work.
- Family pooled money for funeral costs.
- Churches passed the hat for rent.
- Friends covered each other's tabs without expecting it back in cash—but maybe in babysitting or gas or showing up when the moving truck pulled in.

This wasn't charity. It wasn't pity. It was the understanding that stability isn't solo.

And the irony? It worked.

It still works—just not in the ways we're taught to value.
Modern Systems Are Built to Shame This

We've been conditioned to believe that real success means never needing help.
But the modern economy has decoupled wages from cost of living.
Healthcare has become unpredictable.
Rents outpace income.
Childcare is unaffordable.

And still we're told: "Just budget better."

But budgeting only stretches so far when the fabric is thin.
That's when mutual aid steps in.

The most financially resilient people don't go it alone.
They build circles.
They circulate resources.
They normalize asking and giving.

Because sometimes the fastest way to keep $200 from becoming $2,000 in debt…
is to let someone loan it to you without judgment.

Bring It Into the 21st Century

We may not live in small villages anymore. But we still know how to show up like we do.

That could mean:

- Creating a group chat with trusted friends to flag urgent needs
- Starting a monthly "emergency round robin" where everyone contributes $50 and one person uses it each month
- Hosting community skill swaps—free haircuts in exchange for résumé help, dog-sitting for tutoring

None of this replaces systemic reform. But while we wait for policy, people can still save each other.

Don't underestimate what small circles can do when they act intentionally.

Use Your Village

You are not weak for needing people.
You are not behind because you asked for help.
You are not a failure because your budget didn't stretch far enough.

You are a human being in a system that wasn't built for your success.

And you still have power.
That power comes from the people you invest in—through trust, care, shared struggle, and real support.
Not everyone will show up. But some will.
Those few? They're your financial superpower.

So build your emergency fund…

but also build your village.
Because when money runs out, it's people who get you through.

Crisis Doesn't Always Look Like Collapse

Sometimes it looks like joy.

We've trained ourselves to see financial crisis in one color: red.
Bank overdrafts. Medical bills. Layoffs. Evictions. We brace
ourselves for collapse, for grief, for loss.

But what if the thing that flips your life upside down doesn't
look like a tragedy?
What if it looks like the best news you've ever received?

We call this good chaos. If you're not ready for it, it can cost you
everything.

Joy Moves Fast, and It Isn't Free

A dream opportunity doesn't show up with a six-month
warning. It knocks on your door with a two-week timeline and
a price tag. A major life event doesn't always let you save up for
it. Sometimes it demands your wallet and your time now—and
expects you to be grateful.

But here's the problem:
If your money is tied up in survival mode or sunk into passive
spending, you don't get to say yes.
You miss the concert. You skip the wedding. You delay the
move.
It's not because you didn't care. It's because you didn't plan for
joy.

You didn't expect the opportunity to cost this much.

Say Yes Without Sinking the Ship

Imagine a close friend announces a destination wedding overseas. The flight alone is over $1,200. The hotel? Nearly $1,000. Add in attire, gifts, meals, and a few days of missed work, and suddenly this celebration costs thousands of dollars.

You love this person. You want to be there. But instead of feeling joy, you're doing math, wondering if you'll have to decline one of the most important moments in their life.

Now imagine you've been steadily building your Resilience Reserve—not just for emergencies, but for opportunities like this.

You check that account and see $6,000 sitting there. Suddenly, you can say yes without wrecking your budget or taking on new debt.

That's emotional freedom. That's what intentional spending buys you—not just protection from collapse, but the ability to fully step into life's invitations without sinking your financial ship.

How to Budget for Joy: The Flexible Plan

The best budgets aren't just spreadsheets. They're ecosystems—with room to grow, to pivot, to breathe.

Here's what that looks like:

1. Add a Joy Line-Item
    If you track spending categories, build one called "Good Chaos." Doesn't matter if it's $20/month or $200/month. Give joy a seat at the financial table. Don't make it beg for scraps.

2. Give Opportunities a Checklist
    When something big shows up, ask:

    - What can I cut immediately to make space?
    - What commitments can I pause?
    - What support can I ask for?
    - What does "enough" look like to make this work?

3. Keep the Decision Emotionally Grounded
    Not every joyful moment is a smart financial decision—but some are worth the stretch. The key is deciding with clarity, not impulse. Ask yourself: Will I regret spending this… or regret not spending it?

A Note on Regret

Regret doesn't only come from what we buy. It also comes from what we missed—the memories we didn't make, the people we didn't show up for, the chances we didn't take.

Financial fear can protect you. But it can also imprison you.
You don't want to be the person who's always too responsible to live.
You want to be the person who's responsible enough to say yes when it matters.

That's what this whole system is about.

Build for the Life You Want

Your spending plan isn't a cage. It's a compass.
It doesn't just tell you what to avoid—it guides you toward
what you value. And value isn't always practical.
Sometimes it's spontaneous. Messy. Beautiful. A little irrational.

Sometimes it's sitting in the airport terminal, passport in hand,
ticket bought with savings you forgot you had, and realizing—I
built this moment. I made this possible. I am not just surviving.
I'm living.

Crisis is simply change at scale.
Your job isn't to avoid it.
It's to be ready when it calls your name—whether it arrives
with a pink slip, a plane ticket, or a second chance.
Not every crisis is collapse.
Some are invitations.
And when those moments come—ready or not—you want your
money to say yes.

Chapter 23: Spending Forward

We have spent the past 22 chapters doing more than just fixing a budget.

We've been building muscle. Pattern recognition. A deeper understanding of why money slips through your fingers and what it means to finally hold onto it with intention. This journey wasn't just about dollars and cents—it was about cost. About truth. About waking up.

Yes, we've talked about recessions. We've talked about debt. About loans and housing and stress and sludge and parents and partnerships and panic. But this isn't a book about fear.

This is a book about power.

We started back at zero—at the cost of doing nothing. That first moment where you realize inaction is a kind of spending. That every time you say, "I'll deal with it later," your finances keep moving… just not in your favor.

From there, we built up to a daily spend mindset—tracking the ways money leaves your life before you even get out of bed. Coffee subscriptions. App renewals. Late-night Amazon scrolls that you forgot until the box showed up. We broke down housing, loans, and education. We called out broken systems. We reminded you—again and again—that this was never just about budgeting.

It was about thinking differently.
It was about seeing spending as a lens. A mirror. A strategy.
It was about giving you a philosophy that doesn't just live in your wallet—it shows up and strengthens your work, your friendships, your career, your community, your country.
This is what I mean when I say: this scales.

The 5 Principles, Reimagined at Full Scale

You now carry five principles that don't just help you spend better… they help you lead better.

Let's revisit them—because now, you get to see what they look like when applied beyond your personal finances.

1. You Spend Money Every Day—Even When You Do Nothing

In your own life, you've learned to track passive spending: unused subscriptions, thoughtless delivery fees, impulse buys. But this isn't just a personal habit—it's a cultural pattern.

Companies lose billions in passive spend every year. Ghost software licenses. Bad contracts. Energy waste. Unused office leases. No decision is still a decision—and it's usually an expensive one.

And governments? They bleed money maintaining outdated systems because overhauls take political courage. They delay repairs until they cost three times as much. They spend to maintain appearances instead of outcomes.

You've learned to fight passive spend in your life. Now ask: What would it look like to fight it at scale?

2. The System Is Designed to Make You Overspend

Once you see the trap, you can't unsee it. Buy now, pay later. Add-ons. Drip pricing. Sludge.

But again—this isn't just your inbox. It's in public procurement contracts. It's in tax loopholes. It's in healthcare billing. It's in student loan servicing. It's in systems that are intentionally complicated so that you default to overpaying, or worse… to giving up.

Recognizing these traps in your personal life prepares you to spot—and challenge—them in the real world. It gives you the tools to question who benefits from confusion. And it teaches you that simplification isn't just a convenience—it's a justice issue. Notice: at scale—just like in your own life—the system never encourages people to ask for help: from government, from community, or from each other. Which is exactly why we have to.

3. Big Purchases Shape Your Financial Future

Whether it's a house, a car, or a degree, you now understand that big purchases aren't just price tags—they're direction-setting events. They shape your flexibility, your freedom, your risk.

Now zoom out: that same principle applies to companies. One poorly timed merger can destroy a decade of progress. One overpriced technology rollout can sink morale and revenue. One unnecessary stadium deal can gut a city's public funding.

Big bets matter. The bigger the system, the bigger the impact of a single choice. That's why the ability to think long-term—like you now do—isn't just personal finance. It's strategy. It's leadership. It's survival.

4. Needing Less Is the Ultimate Financial Power

When you reduce your baseline needs, you gain freedom. You can take a better job that pays less. You can leave a bad relationship. You can take a break. You can breathe.

This is true for organizations, too. The leanest startups don't burn cash trying to look rich—they move fast, adapt, and survive. Cities that invest in efficient transit and walkability don't have to build more freeways. Countries that invest in public health don't need to treat as many preventable diseases.

Power isn't always about acquiring more. Sometimes, it's about needing less. That lesson—more than almost anything—can change the way you live and lead. That's where the next principle comes in—because needing less personally or locally only works if the larger systems around you are built to reinforce the same mindset.

5. Your Community and Government Can Make Life Easier—If You Strengthen Them.

You've now seen how tax systems, subsidies, public programs, and financial policy shape the playing field. Not just for you— but for everyone.

Social Security. SNAP benefits. Public schools.

Libraries. Parks. Transit. Roads.

Healthcare. Clean air. Internet access. Job training. The postal service.
None of it is free. But all of it is shared. It's only ever as good as what we demand from it—and how we support each other in the process.

If you've felt alone in your financial struggles, I want you to remember this: you're not. The systems you've had to fight were designed without you in mind—but they can be redesigned, too. Your new financial literacy makes you not just a better voter or advocate, but a better neighbor and participant in the community that sustains you. Because in the end, leadership isn't about titles or credentials—it's about clarity, contribution, and the courage to strengthen what others depend on. Which brings us to the truth at the heart of this final section: you don't need a degree to think like a leader.

You Don't Need a Degree to Think Like a Leader

There's no diploma at the end of this book.

But if you've made it this far—if you've absorbed these principles, reflected on your choices, and begun to see spending as something worth understanding—you've earned something better than credentials.

You've earned clarity.
You've earned direction.
You've earned a new way of thinking.

You now understand how to evaluate risk.
How to ask better questions.
How to consider cost—not just in money, but in time, in stress, in dignity, in freedom.

That's leadership.

That mindset can live inside anyone—whether you're a parent, a business owner, a teacher, a high school grad, or a community volunteer. This book doesn't care about your income. It cares about your awareness. And now you have it.

The Torch Is Yours

So here's the part I didn't tell you at the beginning:

You were never just fixing your finances.
You were learning how to change the way systems work.

That might mean a business you run someday.
That might mean the way you vote, or the nonprofit you start.
That might mean how you raise your kids or manage your team. That might mean how you advocate for your neighborhood—or how you show up when your neighborhood needs you.

Or how you rebuild your own life, after a setback you never saw coming.

Whatever it is—you're ready.

Because now you don't just know how to spend money…
You know how to spend on purpose.

One Last Thought…

This isn't a finish line. It's the start of a new feedback loop.

You will make mistakes. You'll overspend. You'll trip. You'll get overwhelmed.

When that happens, I want you to treat it like missing a workout, or eating cake when you weren't planning to. That doesn't mean you failed. That just means you need to come back to the plan. Back to your principles. Back to your power.

So if you ever feel lost again—come back here.
To your mindset.
To your strategy.
To your values.
To your voice.

If you want one simple move that will always bring you back on track? Go back to your daily active spend. The same one you calculated early on. Treat it like your anchor. Spend over it today? Adjust tomorrow. Spend under? Bank the extra. That rhythm is your reset button — the fastest way to turn overwhelm into control.

And spend like your future depends on it.

Because it does.

Postscript

Y ou didn't need a textbook.
You didn't need a degree.
You didn't need to be "good with money."

You just needed someone to walk you through it without condescension... and without pretending this was just about cutting back on lattes.

If you made it this far, here's what you've actually done:

- You learned how to budget—but not in the spreadsheet sense. You learned how to see your money clearly.
- You understood debt—but not as failure. As cost. As structure. As reclaimable.
- You grasped housing, education, healthcare, and taxes— not from a political lens, but from a personal one. From lived reality.
- You saw that your spending isn't isolated. It's systemic. The system often counts on your confusion to keep you quiet.
- You picked up terms and ideas that economists spend years trying to simplify: asset bubbles, inflation, compound interest, public goods, subsidies, behavioral nudges, the tax gap. You didn't just memorize them— you felt them. Through examples. Through stories. Through the cost-per-day lens that made it all finally click.

What you just did, without even realizing it, was walk through the core of behavioral finance. That field is usually taught in jargon—anchoring, loss aversion, hyperbolic discounting—but you've been living it in plain English. Every chapter here was about why we spend the way we do, how systems exploit those instincts, and how to reclaim control. That's behavioral finance stripped of the ivory tower.

This wasn't a personal finance book in the way we've been trained to expect.

There were no promises of getting rich. No stock tips. No magic debt payoff plan.

Because this book wasn't about wealth.
It was about your power.

The power to opt out of shame.
The power to ask better questions.
The power to know when you're being manipulated—and how to stop handing over your wallet in the process.

That kind of power is what ended the first Gilded Age over a century ago—when workers, voters, and reformers forced change through trust-busting, labor rights, and progressive taxation. It's the kind of power you need again now to push back against a second Gilded Age quietly unfolding around us.

Along the way, you also learned something bigger — something economists rarely name outright: Economic Distance.

That quiet gap between what your grandparents could afford and what you can't. Between the cost of a home then and now. Between wages that once built stability and wages that now barely buy time.

That distance isn't an accident. It's the cumulative effect of decades of policy choices, tax cuts, deregulation, and corporate design — all pushing the cost of living upward while freezing mobility in place.

But recognizing it is power. Because once you see the distance, you can start to measure it, name it, and close it.

You've spent this book doing just that — tracing how those quiet shifts shape every decision you make and every dollar you spend.

You didn't just learn about money.
You learned to reframe your life around it—with empathy,
strategy, and some very sharp math.

This was always how financial literacy should have been taught.

Big picture, small steps.
Rigorous, but not rigid.
Emotional, without losing clarity.
Honest, without being cruel.
Maybe the most important thing you learned?

You were never bad at money.
You were just never given the full picture.
Until now.

If you remember nothing else from these pages, remember your
daily active spend. One fixed, flexible guide that keeps you
steady no matter what life throws at you. It's not magic — it's
math you can actually live with. It works whether you make
$30,000 or $300,000.

When you picked up this book, it might have looked like a
budget guide. But it wasn't. Not really.

What you've just read is closer to an economics book—the kind
we should have had all along. The kind that doesn't talk down
to you with charts about lattes but explains why your spending
feels rigged, why wealth flows upward like gravity, and why
reclaiming control starts one household at a time.
This wasn't just about money. It was about the power you hold.
The clarity you've earned. Taking back what decades of quiet,
relentless theft stripped from working and middle-class families
like your own.

And it was about community… your community. Because the
knowledge you've gained here isn't only yours. It's something
you carry for your neighbor, your family, your country. You

weren't just learning for yourself. You were building community power too. That's how financial literacy scales. That's how we rebuild—not one budget at a time.

Together.

If it felt different than every other personal finance book you've read, good. That means we're on the right track—rewriting financial literacy the way it should have always been taught.

You've got this.

About the Author

Zack Fields is a former telecom strategist who now writes, speaks, and coaches on financial clarity and economic resilience. After more than 15 years helping corporations understand the market, he shifted focus to helping people navigate it for themselves.

He holds an MBA from UCLA Anderson and a Marketing Management degree from Syracuse University, where he was part of the 2004 national championship lacrosse team… contributing heavily from the sidelines.

He's coached individuals, guest lectured at Penn State, and is building a consulting practice focused on making strategy accessible to underserved communities. His work blends systems thinking with a plainspoken approach to money.

This book was written under the careful supervision of his two cats, Arya and Sweet Pea.

Learn more or get in touch at ZackFields.com.

Author's Note

Thank you to everyone who believed in this project before it was real and thank you, the reader, for listening to my thoughts.